Who Are the Mennonite Brethren?

by Katie Funk Wiebe

Illustrated by
Lois Klassen

KINDRED PRESS
Winnipeg, Manitoba, Canada
Hillsboro, Kansas, USA
1984

WHO ARE THE MENNONITE BRETHREN?

Published simultaneously by Kindred Press, Winnipeg, Manitoba, R2L 1L4 and Kindred Press, Hillsboro, Kansas 67063

Library of Congress Catalog Card Number: 84-082049

International Standard Book Number: 0-919797-31-8

Printed in the United States by Multi Business Press, Hillsboro, Kansas 67063

Contents

72875

Foreword

For anyone to attempt to describe a body of believers with thousands of members from many races and nationalities, spread over several continents, seems to be sheer folly. Friends were slightly amused when I described the task assigned to me by the Board of Christian Literature — to identify and define the Mennonite Brethren for people who are either members or interested seekers. Is it possible to describe an elephant, knowing one can see only a small part of it?

I admit that to describe a church body, balancing the strengths that all members have in common with at least a few weaknesses, is a task fraught with dangers. One reader will be certain to exclaim he or she sees an aspect of our common identity quite differently; and another that the side I picture here can't be seen at all, or should have been hidden. In my research I read as widely as possible to establish a consensus of current views of Mennonite Brethren as reflected in our publications. I also acknowledge that this portrait is neither complete nor fully developed. Some sections are only sketched in; others have shadowy areas because the lighting was dim. But I hope all Mennonite Brethren can point to their face sticking out from behind others who may be strangers to them.

Another question I was often asked as I worked was why define or separate the Mennonite Brethren from other Mennonites? Mountains of books have already been written about Mennonites. Why add another? Won't such a book only further isolate the Mennonite Brethren from other Mennonite groups?

Mennonite Brethren have consistently defined themselves as a separate group and yet a group which is part of two other groups: the Mennonite family and also the mainstream evangelical family. For new growth to occur within the church, the risk of defining must be taken in the hope that it will not stifle spiritual growth, but will reveal new directions more clearly as we learn to know our own identity and to share it freely with others.

I present this short study of the Mennonite Brethren, because I, as a member, like all other members, have the responsibility to define for myself the nature of the church I have chosen to identify with. Like all members, I have the obligation to test its doctrine and teachings against the Scriptures in the interests of personal growth and of the whole body. My concern is that this writing may free the way for others to do the same — and thereby build a stronger body of Christ.

— Katie Funk Wiebe
February, 1984

1
About names, labels and such things

You've got questions about the Mennonite Brethren, and someone told you to read this book. Good idea! Although I don't know what your questions are, by working through the kind of questions other people ask about the Mennonite Brethren, I hope we can answer yours. In each chapter, I'll explain some general ideas, then raise some key issues which aren't easily explained in a few paragraphs, and hope I've said enough to send you to other material listed in this book or to persons who can give you more information.

But there's one matter I need to make clear before we start our conversation. This holds true whether you're interested in joining the Mennonite Brethren Church, whether you feel a need for a refresher course, or whether you're just looking. This concern has to do with names, particularly our name as a denomination.

The full name of the Mennonite Brethren Church is the General Conference of Mennonite Brethren Churches of North

America. That includes some 40,000 people in the United States and Canada, scattered from the East Coast to the West Coast in Canada, and in most of the states west of the Mississippi to the Pacific Ocean as well as in North Carolina in the United States. In addition, there are about 60,000 members in India, Africa, South America, Europe, Japan and Panama. The exact number of Mennonite Brethren in the Soviet Union and the Republic of China isn't certain enough to be counted in this tally, but the estimate is about 55,000 Mennonites in the Soviet Union, of which about 22,000 are Mennonite Brethren.

That long title for a denomination is cumbersome, I know, so we're usually known simply as Mennonite Brethren, often shortened to MBs. For some, the term "MB" represents everything good about being a member of the Mennonite Brethren Church. To them it's a warmer term than the heavy-handed title — a diminutive term of affection which draws together. They like to call one another by that nickname. But I have to admit that others don't like either the long label or the short one and would prefer something less "ethnic" and "denominational." But that's a topic for another chapter. So when you see something written about MBs, it doesn't mean Mostly Beautiful, Muddled Baptists or anything like that. It's our name, and some of us like it and some of us don't. It's more important for you to know that we are evangelical Christians who happen to be called Mennonite Brethren because of events in our history.

We never named ourselves. Like the names of some other denominations, our name was first a derogatory nickname that stuck. You'll recall from the book of Acts that scoffers first labeled Christ-followers "Christians" at Antioch. Likewise, a group of radical reformers were first termed "Mennists" in the early 1500s by their adversaries as a term of derision. They had no use for them or for their leader, Menno Simons, a former Catholic monk of Friesland, now known as Holland, who had become dissatisfied with the state church.

Mennonite Brethren, one of many branches of Mennonites, were mocked with the term "brethren" because the founding group members called each other "brother" and "sister" when they seceded from the mother church in the Ukraine, in southern Russia, in the middle of the 19th century (How they got to Russia is part of another chapter). One of the factors in this secession, as we shall see later, was the influence of a pietistic revival conducted by a non-Mennonite preacher, actually a Lutheran. The secessionists left the church in which they had grown up because they considered it unspiritual — unbrotherly and unsisterly. Their hope was to bring into their group a spirit of new life which would make them all brothers and sisters in the Lord, terms still used generously today, especially by the older generation. However, the ones judged to be unbrotherly responded with a taunt. In time, the Mennonite Brethren accepted the "generic" term "Mennonite" and the nickname "brethren" and became known as the Mennonite Brethren.

The label "Mennonite" is very broad, covering a large number of groups which total about 698,300 people organized into 130 bodies in fifty-two countries (1983 figures). Mennonites live in every major population center in the United States and Canada — although not every city has a Mennonite congregation. By continent, North America continues to have the largest Mennonite population, at 329,000. Conversely, that means that over half of the world's Mennonite and Brethren in Christ members, about 369,000, live outside of North America. Non-North American countries with the largest figures are Zaire, 64,408; Indonesia, 52,294; India, 43,802; Mexico, 28,318; and The Netherlands, 22,500. The fastest growing congregations are in Africa and Indonesia. The province of Quebec in Canada is experiencing some extraordinary growth also. At the end of this chapter I'll list for you the names of some of the main Mennonite groups.

"If you're a Mennonite, why don't you wear black stockings and an apron?" a third grader questioned my young daughter a number of years ago shortly after we moved into a community where many plain folk live. We chuckled when a perplexed daughter reported the conversation at the dinner table. She didn't know about these other kinds of Mennonites, as that other little girl didn't know about the many other kinds of Mennonites, like the Mennonite Brethren. Our daughter's new friend had only learned to know the Amish and Old Order Mennonites, with their black stockings, beards, bonnets and buggies.

The Amish, Hutterites and Holdemans are often identified

by the secular press as the main Mennonite groups because
their style of clothing, transportation and vocational choices
make interesting media copy, but they represent that smaller
percentage of the Mennonite population who chose different
emphases in an earlier period of church history and have continued in those patterns. You can think of Mennonite Brethren
and the Hutterities and Amish a bit like distant kissing
cousins, if you want to.

Mennonites are all somewhat conservative Protestant
groups with varying degrees of emphasis on evangelism, missions and social justice. If we discuss only the identity of the
Mennonite Brethren, one segment of our membership would
probably say they want to be known as anabaptist Mennonites
because they hold to the believers free-church tradition, going
back to the time of the radical reformers of the 16th century.
Such members emphasize doctrines they accepted from the
anabaptists, such as adult believers baptism, infallibility of
Holy Scripture, obedience of the believer to Christ before all
others, the nature and mission of authority, and the peace witness. They believe the church is a covenanting body of believers reborn through the Holy Spirit. The community of believers
constitutes the true and visible body of Christ with a lifestyle
of love.

Another segment of the Mennonite Brethren feels a
stronger affinity with mainstream evangelicalism than with
Mennonite groups. Unsure of how to balance the strong Mennonite Brethren emphases on evangelism and missions with
issues of social justice and peace concerns, they emphasize the
pietistic tradition, which had a large part in the formation of
Mennonite Brethren in Russia. They think of themselves more
like Baptists under a different name and wear the label "Mennonite Brethren" a trifle reluctantly, convinced it smacks of
ethnicity and may be a high wall keeping people from joining
them.

Still others don't use the name "Mennonite Brethren" but
yet are "unashamedly Mennonite Brethren," to quote Tim Geddert, former pastor of the growing Fort McMurray church in
Alberta. States Geddert, "We want the church to be a community — not a program, not an organization, not a social club,
certainly not a building — but a community seeking to com-

municate our commitment to Jesus. We want our relationships, our lifestyles, our priorities, and our allegiances to reflect those of our Leader."

The name question keeps coming up. Does the name represent an ethnic group or a religious group? Most of our leaders
would agree we are not primarily an ethnic group but a denomination with peoples of various ethnic descent among its
membership, the largest group in North America being the
descendants of the German-speaking immigrants from Russia.
Other major ethnic groups represented in the United States
congregations are blacks and Hispanics; in Canada they are
the French-Canadians; and in India, South America, Europe,
Africa, Japan, Indonesia and Panama, the nationals.

So MB can mean almost any racial heritage today. Church
roles include any name from traditional ones like Friesen and
Penner to Bondaroff, Dagenau and Danko. Because ethnic
groups tend to intermarry and sometimes enjoy their own folk
and family festivals, the spiritual heritage may at times become obscured by traces of other languages and dialects, folk
foods and customs, and family-tree exploring. However, if the
name "Mennonite Brethren" evokes an image of clear discipleship and an ethic of love in all relations, we are grateful. So
if someone says, "Ah, Mr. Browning, glad to have you here . . .
that isn't a Mennonite name, is it?" — please forgive. We're
still learning.

This spiritual and ethnic pluralism related to our identity
possibly confuses people inside the church more than those
observing us. Some members see these leftovers of a former
strong ethnic culture and don't know what to do with them.
Those who inherited a Russian-Mennonite background sometimes carry it like a grim burden, others like Stephen Crane's
Red Badge of Courage. Nevertheless, I believe the loyal MB
wears the name "Mennonite Brethren" with humble gratitude
and genuine enthusiasm because of the rich heritage of men
and women who practiced a vigorous brand of Christianity,
first during the Reformation period, then later during the Russian interlude, and still later, here in North America.

In the past, the name "Mennonite Brethren" has meant to
its members the essence of the Good News, the reliability and
final authority of the Scriptures, the necessity of personal faith

in Jesus Christ for salvation, and the urgency to bring the word about that salvation to all humankind. Other aspects of our faith will be mentioned later. If the name doesn't mean that today, the problem is not with the name, but with us, its members.

If what our denomination stands for are your concerns, we invite you to join us, for we believe God has given Mennonite Brethren a share of the task to witness to his power and love in building his kingdom. We want to be faithful to that responsibility and to accept the pruning necessary to bear a spiritual harvest. Canadian pastor James Nikkel has said, "Churches with an ethnic or cultural history are particularly vulnerable to growth barriers. If our roots and heritage do not help us to be faithful to the Scriptures, they will become a barrier to

So Mennonite Brethren can mean almost any racial heritage today. . . .

fulfulling the great commission." Our history has had many glorious moments when we pushed ahead, but there were also rough spots when we neglected to give first place to the dynamic of the Holy Spirit. I'll tell you about that later.

At the end of this chapter you'll find some of the most common acronyms used in the Mennonite family. Consider these like freshman initiation, bothersome at first, but essential to be considered part of the family. I know that to the newcomer these pet names look like a stuttering typewriter, but to the veterans they slip lovingly from the tongue. Use this book, and especially the appendixed material at the end of each chapter, like a Baedeker, or a book on how to learn to know the Mennonite Brethren for less than the price of a steak dinner.

Next, I'm going to give you a condensed version of the main aspects of the Mennonite Brethren Church. We'll discuss together what we say we believe and what others say we believe, what we think is important in church life and polity, and a short review of our history.

We'll also talk about areas in which we have enjoyed visible growth that we're grateful for, and also some of the aspects of our life together we're still a little touchy about. I'll let you know about our taboos, and the areas in which we see the need for vision-building and mind-stretching.

So pour yourself a cup of coffee or get yourself a Coke. I'll try to remember that you're not an old pro at this kind of talk about Christ-believers who happen to be called Mennonite Brethren.

SOME MEMBERS OF THE MENNONITE FAMILY:

MB — Mennonite Brethren

MB GENERAL CONFERENCE — The entire North American denomination, as well as the triennial convention.

MC — Mennonite Church, formerly known as the Old Mennonites, now the largest Mennonite body.

GC — General Conference Mennonite Church, the second largest group.

KMB — Krimmer Mennonite Brethren, a group originating in the Crimea, in southern Russia, which merged with the Mennonite Brethren in 1960 after a hundred years as a separate group. Many former KMBs are now MBs, so the term is common.

EMB — Evangelical Mennonite Brethren.

EMC — Evangelical Mennonite Conference, formerly *Kleine Gemeinde*.

EMMC — Evangelical Mennonite Mission Conference, formerly Rudnerweider Mennonite Church.

CGCM — Church of God in Christ, Mennonite, or the Holdemans.

BIC — Brethren in Christ.

2
What Mennonite Brethren believe

You may have noticed that some denominations emphasize creedal statements, first carefully formulating them and then frequently reciting them as an act of worship. Others have no creeds and hold that the New Testament is a sufficient rule of faith and practice for the sincere believer. Under the guidance of the Spirit, she or he will be led aright in interpreting the Word of God and needs no human formulations to set the tone.

Mennonite Brethren come somewhere between these two extremes. They have a *Confession of Faith*, which is revised from time to time, and which differs from a creed in that it does not identify what should be believed, but rather what is believed. You will probably be referred more often to the Scriptures than to the *Confession of Faith* for direction as to what MBs believe. Our very earliest forebears in Europe, however, identified themselves through position papers and confessions of faith, one of the first ones being the Dordrecht Confession of 1632. The Mennonite Brethren adopted an 1853 edition of the West Prussian Mennonite Church Confession, first published in Holland in 1660. About the turn of the century a new version of the confession of faith was drawn up, approved by Mennonite Brethren in Russia and North America, and finally produced in printed form in 1902. This statement was revised in 1966 and again in 1975. "The little green book," as it is sometimes referred to, is used mostly as an outline for biblical instruction, to develop our theology, to clarify church polity (governance) and to direct church disciplinary matters.

Early Mennonite Brethren were much concerned that their doctrine should be based on the Bible as the authoritative Word of God. The first members regularly carried a Bible with them, met often for Bible study, and avidly memorized Scripture passages. When someone had a problem, the group discussed it with a Bible open before them to turn to for principles of guidance. To understand the meaning of Scripture for their time was important."What does the Bible say?" was a common response to questions of faith and practice.

Thus, Mennonite Brethren are known as biblicists, an emphasis which has had far-reaching consequences. At first, the frequent gathering for Bible study (rather than for preaching services) encouraged inquirers to air their questions freely, and when they were answered, to become Christ-followers. In later years, in America, the emphasis influenced the founding of many small local Bible schools which operated in the winter months for lay students of all ages. It also resulted in local congregations sponsoring many local Bible conferences, held for days or weeks, to instruct in the Word and to achieve consensus on the interpretation of difficult passages. The emphasis on Christian education in the congregations and the establishment of church-related high schools and colleges can also be attributed to this stress on the need to know the Word of God.

Mennonite Brethren accept that the church, the community of faith, is an interpreting community. This means that the congregation as a body seeks out the truth of Scripture under the leadership of Bible scholars, with each member free to offer his or her view of the meaning of the passage. This consensus approach to Bible interpretation guards against the kind of subjectivism which permits each member to decide individually what he or she believes.

At this point I should explain briefly the difference between a doctrine and theology, both of which appear in a statement of faith. At times the two terms are used almost interchangeably. While they are always the same to a degree, they mean different things. Doctrine is the straightforward teaching of the Bible on any subject, such as the nature of God, sin, salvation and so forth. It usually varies little from generation to generation. Theology, expressed in confessions, or statements of faith, may adapt itself to the times, for it is the interpretation of the doctrines to daily life and practice. As culture changes, the application of Scripture to the new situation must be determined. So the theology doesn't really change, but the application of truth to new situations makes it seem as if something is changing with the times. Theology organizes doctrines, shows how they relate to each other and to the times, exposes problems connected with them, and defends their teaching.

On some topics, the Bible is very clear and so the doctrine is also clear; on others, much prayerful thought is required to arrive at the position the church should take; for example, on issues related to human sexuality (divorce, abortion, homosexuality and birth control), or related to militarism, such as joining the military or paying war taxes. The Bible does not say in so many words that birth control, for example, is right or wrong, or whether a person should or should not become a member of the army. So most denominations work together as a body on difficult questions, hammering out a position on which they can agree.

You can see that it is important for the church to be united in its interpretation of the Bible, not only to order its own corporate life, but also to communicate its message to the world. Without such unity, disorder and confusion sets in. Unless Christians constantly work as a body to relate their faith to the specific times in which they live, a spirit which no longer acknowledges Christ as Lord creeps in and saps the life-blood of the church.

The church safeguards its interpretation of the Word by relying on the entire community of believers to come together in prayerful consideration of a Bible passage. When Christians refuse to study the Scripture, or to share with others their insights on what it says, or if they say they are satisfied with the theology already declared and refuse "to do theology" — to think through how to mediate the truth of the gospel to their society — they are evading some of their responsibility as disciples of Christ.

Taking pride in being known as biblicists, but not taking time to study the Scriptures, can lead to the danger of using Scripture to support what we want to see in it while shutting our minds to other truths. White, middle-class Christians in North America are always in danger of disregarding the perspective of other racial, cultural or economic views inherent in Scripture. Mennonite Brethren, who have traditionally stressed crisis conversion, piety (personal religious experience) and evangelism, are especially in danger of using these truths as blinders against what the Scripture also teaches about discipleship, which entails an adequate witness in the social, political and economic arenas of the world.

The first Mennonite Brethren confessions of faith were usually phrased in biblical language. The following statement, which includes the main tenets of Mennonite Brethren doctrine, incorporates a measure of theology, or interpretation of Scripture. For a fuller version, see the *Confession of Faith* (1976) from which the following was condensed. Editions are also available in French and Spanish.

I. God and His Revelation

God is the eternal Spirit who has infinite holiness, power, wisdom, love and mercy. He orders all things in the universe he created to serve his eternal purpose and in a way human beings can know him. God reveals himself as Father, Son and Holy Spirit.

Jesus Christ, the eternal Son of God, was sent by the Father to reconcile a sinful humanity to himself. Conceived by the Holy Spirit and born of the Virgin Mary, he lived a holy and sinless life, was crucified and died for the sin of humankind and rose from the dead. He is now with God the Father, interceding for all who believe in him. He will come again to judge the living and the dead and to establish his eternal kingdom.

The Holy Spirit is one with the Father and the Son. He convicts, regenerates, guides, rebukes, empowers, comforts and unites believers into one body.

Scripture is inspired by God as the writers were moved by the Holy Spirit. Both the Old and New Testaments are the infallible Word of God and the authoritative guide for the faith and life of the Christian. God revealed himself in the Old Testament through words and actions and established a covenant with his chosen people. He revealed himself supremely and finally in Jesus Christ in the New Testament. Christ is the key to understanding the Bible. The Old Testament bears witness to him and the New Testament fulfills this witness.

As you study the following Scriptures, remember they are representative and not exhaustive: Gen. 1; Deut. 6:4-6; Ps. 139; Is. 40; Mt. 28:19; Jn. 1:1,18; 4:24; 15:26; Rom. 8:1-17, 26-27; 2 Cor. 3:17; 5:19; 13:14; Phil. 2:6-8; 1 Tim. 3:16; 6:15-16; Heb. 11:6; Jude 25; Ps. 19; 119:105; Lk. 24:27,44; Rom. 1:18-23; 2 Tim. 3:15-17; 2 Pet. 1:16-21; Heb. 1:1-2; 8:5-13.

II. Humanity, Sin and Salvation

Human beings were created in the image of God, sinless and in fellowship with him, with a free will to make moral choices. When Adam and Eve sinned by willfully disobeying God, they broke fellowship with him, thereby bringing physical, spiritual and eternal death on the whole human race. Consequently, everyone is sinful by nature, guilty before God, and in need of forgiveness.

Jesus Christ is the one mediator between God and humankind. He came to redeem the human race from the judgment and power of sin and to reconcile men and women to God. Through his death on the cross, Christ became the sacrifice which was sufficient to atone for sin and which established God's new covenant with humanity. (Gen. 1:27; 3:1-19; Mt. 19:13-15; Rom. 3:10-18; 5:12; 18:21; Eph. 2:1-3; Acts 2:42,46; Eph. 1:13-14, 2:8-9; 1 Tim. 2:5-6; Heb. 4:12; 9:15-28; 1 Jn. 1:9).

III. The Christian Life

The Holy Spirit lives in every Christian and transforms

him or her into the image of Christ. He empowers the believer to follow Christ and be an effective witness for him. The Christian is expected to live in fellowship with God and other believers and to join a local church at baptism. He or she helps to build the body of Christ with spiritual and material gifts. Nurtured through the Word, fellowship and prayer, the believer grows more Christlike and glorifies God by being a witness for him in everyday life. All followers of Christ continually need the forgiving, chastening and cleansing grace of the Lord. The fruit of the Spirit is increasingly evident in the believer's life, especially in relationship with other people. (Mt. 5:13-16; Jn. 12:26; 15:4-5; Rom. 6, 8:9-16; 12; 1 Cor. 6:19; Eph. 2:1-4; 4:1-16; Tit. 2:11-14; Heb. 12:14; 1 Jn. 3:17-18).

IV. The Church of Christ

The church is one body, consisting of believers from all nations, races and social classes, who have been regenerated by faith in Christ and baptized by his Spirit into one body with Christ as head. God, through the Holy Spirit, gives his children gifts for ministry to build up the body of Christ. Some members receive special gifts for leadership, or for pastoral, preaching, teaching, evangelistic and deaconal ministries. A congrega-

Nurtured through the Word, fellowship and prayer, the believer grows more Christlike. . . .

tion, under the Holy Spirit's guidance, may commission or ordain such servants. (Mt. 18:15-35; Jn. 13:1-17; Acts 2:38-44; 15:1-28; 1 Cor. 12-14; 2 Cor. 2:6-8; Eph. 1:22-23; 2:10-22; 5:21, 25-27; 1 Thess. 5:11, 14; 2 Thess. 3:6, 14-15; Rev. 5:9).

The primary task of the church is to make disciples of all nations. Every member is responsible to witness to the power of God for salvation and to meet the total needs of the person. (Mt. 2:23; 11:5; 28:19-20; Acts 1:8; 2 Cor. 5:18-20).

V. Baptism and the Lord's Supper

Christians should obey their Lord's command to be baptized in the name of the Father, Son and Holy Spirit. Baptism by immersion symbolizes death to sin, resurrection to the new life in Christ, and the acknowledgment of the Holy Spirit's indwelling presence. Baptism is also a public commitment to discipleship. At baptism the believer enters into the full fellowship and work of the church. (Mt. 28:18-20; Acts 2:38; Rom. 6:2-6; Col. 2:12-13; 1 Thess. 5:23-24; 1 Pet. 3:21).

The elements of the Lord's Supper as instituted by Christ symbolize his broken body and shed blood and are a memorial to the believers of his suffering and death. They also express the fellowship and unity of believers with Christ. Participation in the ordinance strengthens Christ's followers for discipleship. (Mt.16:24; 26:26-30; 1 Cor. 10:16-17; 11:23-32; 14:26; Rev. 3:20).

VI. Marriage and the Christian Home

God instituted marriage for the intimate companionship of husband and wife and for the procreation and nurture of children. Those who marry should share a common Christian commitment. A believer should not marry an unbeliever. Divorce constitutes a violation of God's intention for marriage. Christian parents should teach their children the Scriptures, lead them in worship, train and discipline them, and be an example to them of godly living. (Gen. 1:27-28; 2:18-24; Prov. 5:18-19; Mal. 2:13-16; Mt. 5:31-32; 19:4-9; 1 Cor. 7:10-11; 2 Cor. 6:14; Eph. 5:22-23; 6:4; Heb. 13:4).

VII. The Lord's Day and Work

Following the New Testament example, believers come to-

gether on the first day of the week to commemorate the resurrection of Christ and the coming of the Holy Spirit. On the
Lord's Day, believers spend their time in worship and instruction in the Word, fellowship and service. They limit their labor
to necessary work and to deeds of mercy. God intends each
man and woman to work diligently and honestly in his or her
chosen vocation and to build his kingdom through it. (Gen.
2:1-3; Ex. 20:8-10; Mt. 6:33; Lk. 24:1-26; Acts 2:1; 20:7; Rom.
14:5-6; Eph. 4:28; 1 Thess. 4:11-12; Heb. 10:23-25).

VIII. Christian Integrity

Christians speak the truth because they are always in the
presence of God. They affirm the truth in legal transactions
instead of swearing an oath because Christ commanded them
to do so. Membership in lodges and secret societies which re-
quire the swearing of oaths and which foster close alliances
with unbelievers is discouraged. (Mt. 5:33-37; 23:1-12; Jn.
18:19-23; 2 Cor. 6:14-18; Eph. 5:6-13; Jas. 5:12).

IX. The State

God instituted the state to maintain law and order in civil
life and to promote public welfare. Its functions and responsibilities are distinct from those of the church. The primary
allegiance of all Christians should be to Christ's kingdom, not
the state. It is their duty to respect those in authority and to
pray for them. Christians should exercise social responsibility,
witness against corruption, discrimination and injustice, pay
taxes and obey all laws that do not conflict with the Word of
God. (Mt. 22:17-21; Acts 4:19; Rom. 13:1-7; 1 Tim. 2:1-6; 1 Pet.
2:13-14).

X. Love and Nonresistance

Christians should live by the law of love, practicing forgiveness of their enemies as taught and modeled by Jesus Christ.
The church, as a fellowship of redeemed people, is responsible
to present Christ, the Prince of Peace, as the answer to human
need, hostility and violence. The Christian practices this law
of love in all relationships and in all situations, including those
involving personal injustice, social upheaval and international
tension. The evil nature of war contradicts the teaching of

The evil nature of war contradicts the teaching of Christ's love. . . .

Christ's love; therefore, it is not God's will that Christians take up arms in military service, but where possible perform alternate service to reduce strife, alleviate suffering and bear witness to Christ's love. (Ex. 20:1-17; Mt. 5:17-28,38-45; Rom. 12:19-21; 13:8-10; 1 Pet. 2:19-23).

XI. Christ's Final Triumph

God, who acts in history, will bring his purposes to a final consummation. At death the righteous enter a state of rest in the presence of God and in fellowship with Christ; the unrighteous suffer the torment of separation from God while awaiting final judgment. When the Lord returns, living believers will be united with him and the dead in Christ will be resurrected to be with him forever. Christ will judge all people. The righteous will inherit the kingdom of God and the unrighteous will suffer the anguish of eternal hell. In the final end, death will be destroyed and Satan cast into a lake of fire. Christ will create a new heaven and a new earth in which righteousness will reign and God will be all in all. (Is. 2:4; 61:1-11; Mt. 25:13,31-46; Mk. 9:43-48; Lk. 16:22-23; Jn. 5:25-29; Acts 1:11; 1 Cor. 15:21-58; Phil. 1:21-24; 1 Thess. 4:16-17; Tit. 2:11-14; 2 Pet. 3:3-13; Rev. 1:15,20-22).

Theologian David Ewert writes that the *Confession of Faith* is "normative insofar as it represents accurately what the Bible teaches, and is subject to revision if we should receive new light on one or the other article. Until that happens, Mennonite Brethren (if they have integrity) are obliged to hold to our *Confession of Faith*. If there are articles in our *Confession* that a person cannot accept, then he or she should find a church with those teachings he or she can fully agree." These words may sound hard, but it is important for all Christians to find a church home where they are comfortable with the teaching, with the approach to the Word of God, and with the ministry of the church. That's part of the reason we're having this conversation together.

FOR FURTHER READING:

Confession of Faith of the General Conference of Mennonite Brethren Churches. Hillsboro, Kansas: Board of Christian Literature, 1976.

Schmidt, Henry J. *Conversion: Doorway to Discipleship.* Hillsboro, Kan.: Board of Christian Literature, 1980.

3
How we interpret the Bible

As I mentioned in the previous chapter, the way Christians express their beliefs in the home, at work and at leisure constitutes the theology of a religious group. In addition to the influence of each member's personal understanding of the Scriptures and the group's corporate Bible study, the way in which a congregation or denomination translates the Word into life experiences is also affected by the emphases of strong leaders, by the theology of denominations in close contact with its members, by the experiences of the members in relationship to current societal events, and by tradition.

Mennonite Brethren theology has been influenced by three movements, the strongest of which was the spirit of pietism in the 1850s affecting the first members, German-speaking settlers from Prussia living in the Ukraine in Russia. This influence came through the preaching of the popular and powerful Lutheran pastor Eduard Wuest.

The second major influence was the doctrine of the Bap-

tists in Russia and of mainstream evangelicalism (of which
Baptists are a significant part) in North America. Our strong
emphasis on baptism by immersion, for example, came partly
through the writings of Ann Judson, wife of Adoniram Judson,
Baptist missionaries of the early 19th century, which early
Mennonite Brethren leaders happened to read. At one time, a
few congregations in Russia adopted a Baptist confession of
faith, but it was never accepted by the entire conference of
congregations.

The third major influence on the Mennonite Brethren was
the theology of 16th century anabaptists of Europe and their
emphasis on nonresistance, separation of church and state,
their call for simplicity and nonconformity to the world, and
their practice of mutual aid. Canadian and U.S. Mennonite
Brethren continue to find a source of direction in the writings
of present-day anabaptist theologians.

I have been using the term "pietism" frequently. What
does it mean when I say Mennonite Brethren have been influenced by pietism and are still somewhat pietistic? Pietists acknowledge a personal religious experience and the presence
and activity of the Holy Spirit as the power which revitalizes
and directs their lives. They emphasize that the indwelling
power of the Spirit enables one to become more like Christ.
They hold that the supernatural is a present reality in a believer's life; God lives and works in a believer's life today as
he lived and worked in Bible times.

Early Mennonite Brethren stressed that the Christian life
begins with a struggle against sin and Satan, followed by a
strong sense of conviction, but also of the power of God's grace
to redeem, and finally, by assurance of salvation. They held
that belief means to give mental assent to the facts of the
gospel; faith means to trust in the indwelling Spirit to forgive,
to guide and to be present to strengthen in daily life. Most
Mennonite Brethren still accept these statements as truth.

When pietism becomes extreme (some people call it becoming hyper-spiritual), it may turn into a form of escape from the
harsh realities of life to an inner world of religious experience,
sometimes overcharged with emotionalism and an overabun-
dance of "spiritual" language without the fruits of the Spirit.
To offset these excesses of emotion, a reactionary movement,

leaning toward rationalism, sometimes sets in. Mennonite
Brethren have had several episodes in their early history when
extreme emotionalism took over in their honest yearning for
a stronger religious experience, which led to severe problems
within the congregations and in interpersonal relationships
within the church. You can read about these events in books
like P.M. Friesen's mammoth history of the Mennonite Brethren in Russia before 1910 and in J.A. Toews's *A History of the
Mennonite Brethren Church.*

Piety is usually a word with positive connotations. Pious-
ness, on the other hand, has negative overtones. However, I
have to admit it's a word that has also been applied to Mennonite Brethren. Historian P.M. Friesen, whose name you will
hear quoted frequently, accused the Mennonite Brethren of
the late 19th century of being "artificially pious," or putting on
the face of spirituality. He called this one of the most repulsive
aspects of the church. He encouraged Mennonite Brethren to
become active reconcilers in the faith and admonished them to
remember that membership in the Mennonite Brethren
Church was not "after all synonymous with membership in
God's church, to which all children of God belong." His words
are a good reminder that even though we may have the language and posture of faith, the power of the gospel can still
escape us. Having the form, but not the content, is like carrying water in a sieve.

The influence of the anabaptists and Baptists will be discussed later, so we will move on to the main emphases of Mennonite Brethren theology, or a short discussion of how we interpret the Bible.

I. Biblical Authority

Mennonite Brethren hold that the Bible, being the Word
of God, is the supreme authority on all matters of faith and
practice. Some denominations place ultimate authority in the
head of the church. Mennonite Brethren believe that no person
or group of people is free to propose guidelines for life that
conflict with the teachings of the Scripture. All members need
to keep going back to the Bible to discover its meaning.

Because God is a speaking God, his revelation through
prophets and apostles is both propositional (meaning it is pos-

sible to make specific statements about his nature), and personal (meaning he illumines himself to the individual in meditation and prayer).

The Bible is accepted as the inspired Word of God and the infallible (incapable of error) and inerrant (free from error) rule of faith and life for humankind. This principle of biblical authority (*sola scriptura*) controls the way Mennonite Brethren interpret the Bible. Although each believer will always read and study the Bible from his or her own stance, there are ways to approach the Bible that aid responsible interpretation. Consider the following:

(a) You, as the interpreter, must always try to understand the original author's intent. Because God revealed himself in history to people with varied personalities living in various cultures, the proper interpretation of the Bible requires an understanding of the cultural context — its language and concepts, the literature and literary forms. Biblical writers did not separate themselves from the culture in which they were living, nor can you in studying their words.

(b) The Old and New Testaments are an organic unity; they form a whole, like an orange or a beautiful piece of art. Because all Scripture is inspired of God, you can expect the parts to harmonize without contradictions and to complement each other despite the diversity of writers. This doesn't mean that biblical harmony implies a mechanical conformity, like the parts of your car engine, but rather that some readers will come to different conclusions on details in their interpretation of some doctrines, such as eschatology (doctrine of last times).

(c) As you study, remember also that God's revelation is progressive, and God's acts in redemption are a chain of events spanning thousands of years. This chain culminated in the incarnation, death and resurrection of Jesus Christ and the further events and interpretations in the New Testament. Both the Old and New Testaments find their central focus in Christ. Old Testament texts or events are referred to in the New Testament with added meanings not apparent in the earlier Old Testament context.

(d) To interpret the Scriptures and respond to them requires that you receive the illumination of the Holy Spirit (1 Cor. 2:12-14). Believers need to seek the help of the Spirit to

The Old and New Testament form a whole, like an orange or a beautiful piece of art. . . .

apply the Word of God to the present situation, whatever it may be.

(e) Any interpreting of Scripture you do needs to be done with a right attitude within the believing community, not only alone. The Bible encourages believers to hunger and thirst for God, his Word and his righteousness, and to meditate on the Word, to seek him in prayer, and to obey his voice. The Bible also underscores the interdependence of the members of the body of Christ in understanding the Bible and how it contributes to one another's growth. The congregation as a body interprets the Scriptures; the community of faith, which includes every member of the congregation, old and young, rich and poor, male or female, is therefore an interpreting community.

II. Conversion

Conversion, or the new birth, is one of the most developed aspects of Mennonite Brethren theology. Pastor Wuest, the Lutheran revivalist in Russia, preached the new birth as a real experience of salvation through Jesus Christ. It released the seeker from the conviction of guilt, granted a sense of peace with God and persons, and gave purpose and direction for life. Few conversion stories of the early members exist, but the early emphasis was that conversion had to have a point of beginning, a distinct time of turning around, as opposed to "memorized faith." Evidence of regeneration should be apparent in the new believer's life. Members of this new group wanted to see with their eyes, not just hear words that Christ had entered a person's life. Baptism by immersion and acceptance into the membership of the congregation followed conversion.

When the Mennonite Brethren Church began, conversions were mainly those of adults with adult experiences with sin, so each man or woman often had definite acts of sin to turn from. For many decades, church leaders attempted to standardize conversion to a time, place, day and assurance through some Scripture verse. You will soon discover that this em-

Conversion means a conscious turning to Christ and away from sin. . . .

phasis to have all experiences conform to a certain pattern is not as strong today. Conversion is seen as the act of making a definite covenant with God in the context of the church. The individual is expected to give evidence by word and deed of the decision to accept God's redeeming grace and become a disciple of Christ. Children are regarded as covered by Christ's atoning work until they are morally responsible for their own decisions.

Here are a few terms you can expect to hear in Mennonite Brethren circles: *Conversion*, as already stated, means a conscious turning to Christ and away from sin. Therefore, infant baptism is rejected and only those capable of professing faith are accepted as candidates for baptism. *Salvation*, the beginning of the Christian life, and *growth in Christ* are an integral unity, for upon acceptance of Christ by faith, the Holy Spirit comes to indwell the believer, serving thereafter as a guide to right living and leading the believer into his truth. *Regeneration* is the basic change in the believer by the power of the Holy Spirit, which affects the mind, will, emotions, attitudes and relationships. The process of becoming like God, or becoming "holy," is known by the term *sanctification*. We don't think of it as a second blessing, as some denominations define it, granted to the believer apart from the new birth, nor as a non-blessing, never in evidence.

III. Discipleship

Faithfulness in following Christ was not a new teaching for the Mennonites who left Prussia for Russia about 1800 (explained in Chapter 9), but they became lax in stressing the need for high standards of ethical living as examples of Christ's indwelling power. Some of the first church schisms in Russia came about because of the insistence of some members that a Christ-follower should show a sense of new direction after being converted. Worldly standards of success and morality should not mold their lives. Some members were particularly upset by the drunkenness and immoral living of members who participated in communion. They maintained that to follow Christ meant to live a distinctively Christian life in relationship to family, neighbors and the state. Each church member was responsible to the entire body for his or her behavior, and

if upon repeated loving admonition persisted in sinful practices, was subject to discipline and possibly excommunication.

Some church historians write that the first Mennonite
Brethren leaders in their zeal for a pure and holy church were
possibly unnecessarily harsh and rigid in deciding what was
outside the bounds of holy living. Once organized as a body,
they sometimes banned members without prayerful delibera-
tion and amid much confusion. Today, Mennonite Brethren
take a more moderate stance toward church discipline and are
slower to excommunicate, upholding biblical guidelines for
holy living rather than making lists of rules and regulations
of what to avoid. The goal is to restore members to fellowship
through loving admonition and counsel rather than through
excommunication.

IV. Evangelism and Missions

Evangelism and missions have been a priority from the
time the church first began. The church grew rapidly at first
from a charter membership of about fifty-four in 1860 to
600 in 1912. The first overseas missionaries were sent from
Russia in 1890, a move followed by continuous interest in and
support of overseas missions as well as concern for home mission endeavors and evangelism. At first, some of the new Mennonite Brethren settlers in America, after the immigration to
that country in the 1870s, had a marked concern that
evangelism of next-door neighbors in America might taint the
church and bring into their midst people who didn't understand their strong concern for purity of life and doctrine.
Today, however, attitudes are changing; Mennonite Brethren
are concerned that the church fulfill Christ's command to reach
all people with the message of the gospel. We're happy for the
new emphasis.

V. Church

When believers join the church, they become part of a family of God in which each member is responsible for others out
of love for Christ. The MB Church developed over 120 years
ago partly as a reaction to authoritarianism in the leadership.
Its early strength was "brotherhood," or community, with no
social classes and no distinction between those preaching the

Word and those hearing it. Everyone was a brother or sister in Christ, and, as a member of the priesthood of all believers, each had the right to express his or her faith in testimonies, prayers, visions, calls for intercession and insights from God's Word. All had the responsibility and privilege of showing loving concern for members of God's family and those still outside it.

Not much of that has changed. The church still sees itself as a dynamic fellowship which gives its members a purpose to live for and power to live by. The local congregation is a redemptive fellowship with a sense of mission and concern for one another's needs — spiritual, emotional and physical. Yet each local body is also well aware that it is an imperfect fellowship, daily facing Satan's attempts to break its unity and weaken its witness, and that it needs the grace, mercy and love of God in Christ to keep it faithful and pure.

FOR FURTHER READING:

"How We Interpret Scripture" in the *Christian Leader*, Aug. 29, 1978.
    This statement was presented by the Board of Reference and Counsel to the General Conference of Mennonite Brethren Churches at Buhler, Kan., 1978.

4
The ties that bind

You will find that in our congregations faith is presented as having several facets. From one viewpoint, it is an individual commitment to God through Jesus Christ as Savior and Lord and to becoming a member of the Christian church worldwide. From another viewpoint, it is also a commitment to a local congregation of believers. An essential aspect of the gospel is the creation of a community of believers, calling them out from the kingdom of the world into the kingdom of God. Once a person becomes a believer, he or she is expected to find a congregation of believers to worship and serve with. Though you will find a strong push in an individualistic society to bypass the other members of the family of God and head straight for him, Mennonite Brethren hold that salvation is faith in God, but also identification with God's community. You can't be a Christian in isolation. To remain a vibrant, growing Christian, and to fulfill Christ's commission to take the gospel to all lands, you need other believers.

The Bible has nothing to say concerning churches as denominations, but it has a great deal to say about the church of Jesus Christ, meaning the whole body of believers. But for convenience and because of doctrinal differences, sometimes quite slight, and sometimes because of human frailties, Christians have organized into groups which we know by denominational names.

Congregational life and work has always been an important part of being a Mennonite Brethren. Our early forebears were teasingly called "brethren" because they set the priesthood of all believers before ecclesiastical hierarchies. Some members still like to use the term "brotherhood" to refer to members because of its warm, family implications, even though today it has some gender connotations and is being replaced with "community," "peoplehood" and "family of God." When believers join the church, they become part of a Christian family in which each member carries responsibility for all other members, including decision making. The freedom to join in decision making is, however, coupled with the obligation to follow the entire body in its vision and decisions whether one agrees or disagrees with them.

This basic view of the corporate Christian life is also the basis for the way Mennonite Brethren congregations function today. Though spread far and wide geographically, we opt to function as one body in many aspects of our denominational witness. You, as an individual Christian or the congregation with which you worship, are not expected to stand alone. All are invited to join spirit, gifts and energy at various conference levels to extend the kingdom of God. Uniting all Canadian and United States congregations is the General Conference of Mennonite Brethren Churches, which convenes every three years in a different locality so that more members can attend. Member churches are expected to support conference activities, recognize and abide by all conference resolutions, and carry them out to the best of their abilities.

In the early years the General Conference had numerous authoritative leaders, an ethnic tradition and a task to perform, particularly in missions and education. The ethnic tradition has subsided into the background and leaders have changed, but the task remains the same — to carry the mission of the church forward, particularly through missions and various educational institutions.

Some leaders see the General Conference developing more like a federation of two national conferences (the Canadian and the United States Conference) than as one large body. The Canadian body convenes annually and the United States body convenes triennially for inspiration and nurture and to regulate other levels of activity. The third level of conference activity is regional — the provincial conferences in Canada and the district conferences in the United States. Again, each has specific assigned areas of responsibility.

Through boards and committees, the General Conference promotes the spiritual life of the entire body of churches and establishes and watches over church doctrine and polity. The Board of Reference and Counsel, responsible for the spiritual watchcare of all congregations, occasionally convenes study conferences on current issues, like hermeneutics (principles of biblical interpretation) and eschatology (the end times). The Board of Missions and Services directs all mission and service activities to meet the spiritual and material needs of people in overseas countries. The Board of Christian Literature supervises the publication of materials to extend and strengthen faith and witness in printed form. The Board of Trustees transacts all legal and business affairs for the General Conference, watches over all property, makes investments and promotes stewardship.

The largest of the national conferences is in Zaire, with about 35,000 members. Other national conferences, in addition to the Canadian and United States conferences, have been organized in India, Europe, Japan and South America. Each is responsible for home mission efforts, Christian education, evangelism, higher education, youth and camp work, music and publication efforts relating to their geographic area and their ability to meet the need.

In the United States and Canada, each conference in turn is divided into regional conferences, either by groups of states or by provinces. The U.S. Conference has the following district conferences: Southern, Central, Pacific, Latin America (LAMB), and North Carolina. In Canada, division is by provinces: British Columbia, Alberta, Saskatchewan, Manitoba, Ontario, and Quebec. There is also one congregation in the Maritime provinces. Each conference is responsible for home mission efforts, Christian education, evangelism, higher education, youth and camp work, music and publication efforts relating to their geographic area as they see the vision and feel able to meet the need.

The relationship between the local church and the conference at all levels is both close and yet relaxed. Each church is self-supporting in the management of its affairs, but all congregations that belong to the conference attempt to "keep the unity of the Spirit in the bond of peace" (Eph. 4:3) and to "walk by the same rule" (Phil. 3:16). Each local congregation is self-governing, but respects this autonomy as something which can only be exercised in relation to other churches within the conference. Affiliated churches at every level are expected to support conference activities, recognize and abide by all conference resolutions, and carry them out to the best of their abilities.

In the administration of local affairs, each congregation handles its own matters without conference interference. If any problem cannot be solved or handled alone, it can solicit help from the next level in the conference structure. When a church is unsuccessfully battling difficulties from within or without its membership, the Board of Reference and Counsel steps in in a supportive way to bring new strengths and insights to the problem. Mennonite Brethren began, in part, as a reaction to the authoritarian way a hierarchy of elders set policy and controlled the congregation in a formal manner. Today they therefore aim for a more congregational style of governance.

Why have so many different levels of conference structure? Why not just function as independent congregations without ties to other bodies? The answer is simple. Because the act of visibly belonging to one another strengthens our vision of the task and unites us. One of the other congregations or conferences may have a clearer, fresher vision of an aspect of the Lord's work. Working together means that the vision can be passed on to others. Also, a conference combines efforts and makes it possible to accomplish tasks individual congregations couldn't even consider. It is more profitable and efficient to work together.

If you get an opportunity to attend a convention session, you will find that delegates and guests spend considerable time listening to reports of how Mennonite Brethren have fared in the last interim, and then in weighing the reports and agreeing upon the challenges for the coming interim. But time is also spent in worship and thanksgiving and in learning to know one another better as members of the same denominational family. Often those present join in communion to witness to their unity in Christ. Going to conference is a longstanding tradition for some people; they need this periodic shot in the arm as if prescribed by a doctor — and the convention also needs them.

So when you contribute time, spiritual and physical energy, and economic resources to the church, you are investing in a worldwide ministry together with thousands of other Christians in other congregations. At the local level you sup-

When you contribute time, spiritual and physical energy, and economic resources to the church, you are investing in a worldwide ministry. . . .

port local operations and ministries. Through your gifts to your congregation's budget, you make it possible for regional conferences to start new churches and assist young ones, to support summer camps, Christian education efforts and the ministry of district ministers who help congregations find pastors and work through difficult issues.

At the national level (U.S. and Canada), you support institutions and agencies directed by these national conferences, such as colleges, publications, youth work and media ministries. At the General Conference level, your donations (also made through your local church budget) send out several hundred missionaries, Christian Service workers and Good News Corps to some two dozen countries to undertake church planting, education and medical and agricultural aid. You also make it possible for men and women to attend the Mennonite Brethren Biblical Seminary, many of whom will work in our congregations and missionary program. The Board of Trustees, which functions something like a savings and loan enterprise, loans funds to churches, conference schools, pastors and missionaries for various projects. But everything starts with you and the other members of your local congregation. You are the keystone of the entire work of Christ. Through your efforts and your gifts, you're undergirding a vast enterprise in the service of God.

SOME EXTRA HELP:

BOMAS: Not a pacifist bomber, but the Board of Missions and Services at the General Conference level. This is one of our oldest boards and carries much responsibility.

BORAC: Not a kind of laundry detergent, but the highly respected Board of Reference and Counsel, which has its watchful eye over the spiritual life of the entire body of Mennonite Brethren.

BCL: Board of Christian Literature. Their responsibility is publishing, a job they do well.

GENERAL CONFERENCE: Not to be confused with the General Conference Mennonite Church, a different branch of Mennonites. When we say "General Conference" it can mean the entire denominational association, or the triennial convention of the United States and Canadian churches.

5
What it means to be a member of a local congregation

I started out this conversation with you on the assumption you are an inquirer or perhaps an old-timer looking for a refresher course in Mennonite Brethren identity. The question before us now is why become, or remain, a member of a local congregation, whether it be a large church with hundreds of members or a small group starting out with only a few families.

Joining a local congregation is a longstanding practice with believers in Christ Jesus. Since, through the gospel, they partake of one Spirit, they also join themselves visibly with other Christians. In the days of the apostles, it was simple to choose a group of believers to worship with, for the church was divided only geographically, with one body at Jerusalem, another at Corinth, still another at Rome and so on. Today the choice is more difficult because Christians are divided by dogma and practices; some denominations minimize denominational membership and stress only the necessity of belonging to the large invisible body of Christ. Mennonite Brethren, with other Mennonite bodies, believe church membership is never something to be taken lightly or loosely. To forego joining a local congregation limits one's understanding and experience of the full love of God.

Church membership begins with the choice to become a believer in Christ, be baptized and be accepted into a local fellowship. We are a priesthood of believers with no distinction between ministers and lay people regarding their position before God. "You are a chosen race, a royal priesthood, a holy nation, God's own nation," wrote Peter (1 Pet. 2:9). As Mennonite Brethren, we have no priests, popes, archbishops, or cardinals who serve as mediators between God and the people. No minister has power that is not equal to the power of the church member. The clergy as a body set apart with special privileges is not inherent in Mennonite Brethren polity. Every person has the right to approach God him or herself.

All actions of a local congregation are determined by that body. While we have denominational offices in Winnipeg, Man.; Fresno, Calif.; and Hillsboro, Kan., nobody or no group can decide for the local church what it should do. It is expected to support the doctrine and mission activity of the total body of churches, but each congregation calls and ordains its own ministers with guidance from district and provincial leaders, and determines its own financial affairs and local discipline. So when you become a member you are not joining a group which will dictate to you what you must do. You join a group in which you determine with the others the best decisions for the entire body. When believers join the church, they become part of a Christian family in which each one carries concern and responsibility for the others. While the church is part of the community, it draws its ethical standards and values from the Bible, rather than from the practices of secular society, to define with others the best ministries that particular group can engage in.

After you are baptized in a local congregation, you will be

When believers join the church, they become part of a Christian family in which each one carries concern and responsibility for the others. . . .

expected to affirm a covenant of your support of the church and its ministries and the standards of behavior expected of children of God. The first Mennonite Brethren congregation in southern Russia probably had few stated requirements for membership other than acceptance of Christ as Lord, baptism and a willingness to live a new life in Christ. Because these founders had a serious concern about laxity of morals, expectations of new members were high, especially with regard to certain forms of behavior, such as drinking, dancing and immorality. These expectations, among others, were gradually codified and passed at district, provincial and General Conference sessions.

Through the decades the General Conference has tried hard to determine the shape of the "new life in Christ." Past resolutions reveal the large amount of time and energy spent on clarifying the "rules" under which members should conduct themselves, some of which make for interesting reading today. In the early years, the conference frowned upon such things as carrying life insurance (1897), joking and jesting among members (1900), attending circuses and theaters (1897) and women worshiping without proper head covering (1878).

One of our senior pastors, Marvin Hein, writes we should not infer that such rules and principles came about by chance or whimsy, but, on the contrary, were hammered out together on the basis of some deep underlying theological principles. "Our earliest churches were born and nurtured in a strongly homogeneous culture. As a result of this tightly knit form of living, economic, social and religious principles were not the choice of the individual but of the corporate body. Corporate or group action governed most of the ethical and spiritual practices of Mennonite Brethren at the time of our denomination's founding." The charter members of the church stressed that individual norms of behavior should be subordinate to the judgment of the entire body.

Clearly, a congregation has some expectations of you as a church member because the Bible calls for a holy, disciplined life. These standards are not requirements for membership or intended to be an uncomfortable weight on you. We're aware that outward conformity to rules and regulations does not prove that a person is acting morally. The early Puritans struggled with maintaining the view that outward evidences proved the validity of an inner commitment to God. We also recognize that by some items in our catalog of sins — drinking, smoking, dancing, gambling — we may be misunderstood as being rigid legalists who contend that goodness or Christlikeness consists of abstinence. Yet as long as we are human, we will need some guidelines, especially with regard to lifestyle issues; to personal relationships in the family, the congregation, at work and in other situations; to relationship to the government, and so forth.

We have not always successfully dealt with all problems on the growing edge of the church. We know there are mediocre Mennonite Brethren, but other denominations struggle too with similar levels of "underachievement." But that's no excuse. If a church is powerless because discipleship has been neglected, the witness of Christ suffers. If you and I identify with Mennonite Brethren, the reason is not because it is the only body of believers or even the best, but because it is our church and its spiritual heritage has nurtured our lives. If we call it ours, we are responsible to question it, even as we are responsible to give it our loyalty and to serve it. I have less responsibility to question other Mennonites, other Protestants or Catholics.

We know from a sociological study of the beliefs, attitudes and practices of the five largest Mennonite and Brethren in Christ denominations that Mennonite Brethren concerns regarding nonresistance, race relations, and social witness are lower than some would like them to be. Our rankings were high, however, in areas of personal devotion and biblical knowledge. I think you'll find that we describe ourselves as people who once were mostly farmers, but who have made the transition to the city, where we're trying to find the best way to be a witness and to begin new communities of believers in obedience to Christ's command. We have strong mission and educational efforts. We are sometimes seen as strongly individualistic in our church programs and relationships with other denominations, but we're learning interdependence. Like many other denominations, which started out with an immigrant base, one of the goals of many members was to take full advantage of the tremendous economic, educational and social opportunities of this land. So we need help in working through a theology of affluence. What does God expect of us with regard to stewardship of our material resources, our talents, our energies, our zeal and ability to pick up big challenges?

What does it mean, then, to be a church member? The congregation has certain responsibilities to you, its member, as you have to other members. They support you and your family in time of sorrow and difficulty as you are expected to comfort others. The congregation's leaders provide you with sound teaching and offer opportunities to join others in Bible study and prayer. You will be given opportunities to share your gifts of time, energy, money and influence with the other members or in ministries beyond the church. All members promise to give each other loving admonition when they stumble in the Christian way, but also to encourage one another in discipleship to Christ. They challenge you to add your strength to the mission of the church and to know the rewards of faithful service.

FOR ADDITIONAL READING:
Janzen, A.E. and Herbert Giesbrecht. *We Recommend... Recommendations and Resolutions of the General Conference of the Menno-*

nite Brethren Churches. Hillsboro, Kan.: General Conference of Mennonite Brethren Churches, 1978. This compilation of resolutions and decisions made by the General Conference from 1878 will give you an excellent overview of the issues which have been considered important to the Mennonite Brethren and how some of these have changed.

Becoming Disciples: A Manual for Church Membership Classes, rev. ed. Hillsboro, Kan.: General Conference of Mennonite Brethren Churches, 1973.

6
Our symbolic acts of witness: Baptism and communion

You're probably aware that all religions have some basic elements in common, just as all plants or animals that belong to a certain family have certain traits in common. According to Eugene Nida, a leading missionary linguist and translator, three essential ones are the practice of religion, the beliefs underlying religious practice, which usually derive from religious practice, and ethical behavior which is validated by religious practice and belief. We've already briefly discussed our beliefs as Mennonite Brethren and something about how they affect our daily lives. Religious practice, which Nida states is at the core of religion, consists of communication to and from God, or more simply prayer and fellowship with him and he with us, and of reenactments of God's communication with his people, such as the Passover of Judaism or the communion of New Testament believers.

With few exceptions, groups of people who call themselves Christians and who come together as the church, the body of Christ, choose to reenact or observe several symbolic practices of faith in Christ Jesus. The two chief observances are the Lord's Supper and baptism. Denominations may not agree completely on the meaning of these observances and may differ also in the manner in which to conduct them, but all regard them as important to the faith and life of the believer.

Some denominations refer to these practices as sacraments, others as ordinances. The word "sacrament" contains the idea of mystery and that the act of participation conveys spiritual merit or Christian virtue. Because of this, a priest or ordained person must be present to conduct the sacrament. Mennonite Brethren and other Protestant groups refer to baptism and the Lord's Supper as ordinances, meaning they are prescribed by Christ and established by the church as ceremonies symbolic of deeper truths. They convey no special spiritual grace upon the participant, yet the act of participation, if entered thoughtfully and with full awareness of its meaning as identification with Christ, his gospel, and the church, can make a difference in how the person thinks about himself or herself, the church of Christ, the Holy Spirit and God.

The first of these ordinances, believer's baptism, is one of the important convictions and practices of the Mennonite Brethren. Baptism, a key issue in religious circles for centuries, was one of the reasons Conrad Grebel, church reformer in Europe in the 16th century, and his friends broke away from Ulrich Zwingli and the state church in Switzerland. It was also one of the key concerns in the origin of the Mennonite Brethren Church in 1860 in South Russia. The questions then were who and by what method should a person be baptized. Simply stated, the issue was what is the meaning of Christian baptism. It is still the main issue regarding baptism today.

At the time of the Reformation, the Catholic Church taught that baptism was essential to salvation and washed away inherent sin. Therefore, to ensure all infants of eternal salvation, baptism was administered as soon after birth as possible, for without it the child was considered eternally lost. Baptism became, over a period of time, the means of incorporating the individual into the general Christian society. In southern Russia, in the middle of the 19th century, even though infants were not being baptized, young people were being integrated into the Mennonite community by means of baptism, for without it the young person couldn't marry or become a full-fledged citizen of the community able to own land and to vote. Baptism was the expected rite of passage for every young person on the way to adulthood. It had lost its spiritual significance and taken on folk values.

During the ensuing Eduard Wuest revival, which was a strong factor in the movement which led to the origin of the Mennonite Brethren, some people insisted that baptism should not be a matter of tradition, parental influence or church or state law. Scripture taught clearly that every person submitting to baptism should do so freely with full understanding. Obviously, infants were incapable of making decisions of repentance and faith. Mennonite Brethren, therefore, accepted anew that believers baptism is the touchstone, or distinguishing mark, of the free church. It publicly announced to the world the believer's separation from the world and his or her commitment to Christ. In anabaptist times, because a decision to be rebaptized upon one's faith was frequently followed by persecution, economic hardships and perhaps martyrdom, only mature people were encouraged to make this commitment.

Mennonite Brethren refuse to baptize infants or very small children who cannot profess faith in Jesus Christ with a full understanding of the commitment they are making. Infants are sometimes dedicated in a public service to give parents an opportunity to openly acknowledge their intention to bring up their children in a Christian environment. Because Mennonite Brethren think of the church as a community of believers, membership is counted only from among those who have been baptized.

Baptism does not wash away sin, nor is it a church social event or some magical rite conveying spiritual grace. Without a previous acknowledgment of sin, repentance to God and acceptance of Christ as Savior and Lord, baptism can have no meaning. Faith in Christ as Lord of life always precedes true baptism. Whereas conversion is a personal, individual matter between God and the believer, baptism is a public affair, an open declaration of faith and allegiance to Christ symbolizing the inner change. You may want to think of it as saying openly to family, friends and others, "I'm now on the side of Jesus Christ. I give him my allegiance."

Candidates for baptism in Mennonite Brethren congregations are expected to tell their pastor, often also the church council and congregation, their spiritual experience and why they would like to be baptized. They are then recommended for baptism if the examining body agrees there has been a genuine turning to Christ. Occasionally some persons may be advised to wait a little longer until their understanding of their relationship to Christ, the church and the world becomes clearer.

Some denominations baptize by sprinkling or pouring, others by plunging the candidate into the water forwards or backwards. Some immerse once, others three times. Some prefer running water, others accept a baptismal font. Mennonite Brethren practice baptism by immersion, usually in a font, although in earlier years candidates were often baptized in a river, lake or reservoir.

At first, Mennonite Brethren required those who wanted to join the church but who had been baptized by some other mode to be rebaptized by immersion. At present, if the person was baptized upon her or his faith, mode of baptism is not an issue; some members, however, believe that immersion best symbolizes the burial of the believer with Christ and resurrection into a new life.

Today there is no specific age at which a person may be baptized. When children have advanced so far they can understand fundamental truths of Scriptures, they may be baptized. A common age for baptism of between twelve and seventeen seems to be developing within the church family with fewer very young children asking to be considered candidates.

Usually immediately after the baptismal service, or later on the same day, the candidates are accepted into full fellowship of the church, and the congregation together participates in the Lord's Supper, or communion. Communion is also observed at other times of the year according to the desires of the congregation and its leadership, sometimes once a month, quarterly or less frequently.

Like the ordinance of baptism, the meaning of the Lord's Supper had a significant part in the origin of the anabaptist movement and later, in the origin of the Mennonite Brethren. In Holland, in the early 16th century, the priest Menno Simons was troubled whether the bread and wine were actually changed into the body and blood of Christ and had an inherent spiritual value. He finally decided after studying the Scriptures that this doctrine was not biblical.

In Russia, in 1860, a small group of believers, concerned about the spiritual laxity in the church, felt they couldn't partake of the Lord's Supper in a setting which included unregenerated church members. When they asked for and were refused the privilege of observing the Lord's Supper as a private group, they observed it among themselves. This act was seen as a stance of defiance and caused a great commotion in the mother church and hastened the formation of the Mennonite Brethren Church.

The way the earlier anabaptists of the 16th century viewed the Lord's Supper influenced the Mennonite Brethren interpretation. The anabaptists (or rebaptizers), often worshiping in caves or hidden places because of fear of persecution, regarded the partaking of the bread and wine as an act done in remembrance of the death of Christ and as a symbol of their togetherness, or unity, in Christ, with each believer being part of the whole.

Mennonite Brethren accepted these two emphases of the Lord's Supper — commemoration of Christ's sacrifice on the cross and a visible reminder to each believer that he or she is a member of a unique fellowship, the company of the redeemed. For this reason, the participation in the Lord's Supper is always a congregational act, not an individual one. For this reason also, the participants must be baptized members of a church, living in a manner worthy of Christ's followers, in good standing with their own congregation. There is no New Testament account of anyone receiving the bread and wine without having professed faith in Jesus Christ, being baptized and being identified with other Christians.

In the early days of the church in Europe and Russia, and

The anabaptists, often worshiping in caves or hidden places for fear of persecution, regarded the partaking of the bread and wine as an act done in remembrance of Christ's death and as a symbol of their togetherness. . . .

also later in Canada and the United States, all nonbelievers were asked to leave before communion was served. During the period of extreme persecution in northern Europe, to participate in communion marked a person as a baptized believer to state authorities. Today, communion in Mennonite Brethren churches is usually open, which means you need not be a member of the congregation where you are participating. People who are not Christians may remain for the service but do not participate.

For sanitation reasons, the common cup is no longer used, and the specific manner in which the supper is observed is determined by the local congregation. At times communion is observed in settings such as retreats, conventions and so forth. It is always, however, expected to be a reminder that the Christian has joined in a new covenant with God in Christ and commemorates the sufferings and death of Christ through the symbols of bread and wine "in remembrance" of him "to show forth his death until (he) comes." God's part of this New Covenant is to provide redemption; our part is to live as disciples under his lordship.

The observance of the Lord's Supper used to be followed by the practice of feetwashing, patterned after Jesus's washing of the disciples' feet (Jn. 13:1-15), shortly before his crucifixion. The Passover feast, a Hebrew celebration, was about to end for Christ's followers with the fulfillment of his death on the cross.

Its regular celebration each year had previously commemo-
rated the act of the angel of the Lord passing over the Israelites
when the plagues afflicted the land of Egypt during Moses's
struggle to liberate the Hebrews from their bondage and bring
them to the promised land of Canaan.

Christ instituted a new memorial in the Last Supper, but
he probably knew his disciples needed something more than a
symbol; they also needed a living example to inspire them during difficult times. So he left the table, laid aside his outer
garments, took a towel and tied it about him, poured water
into a basin and washed his disciples' feet, wiping them with
the towel. All the previous miracles of Jesus had been the
work of One mightier than a human being. This act of washing
the disciples' feet was divine demonstration of a different kind
— a model of how lives transformed by the power of Christ
could become servants of one another. This was the miracle
the disciples could perform daily.

For many decades Mennonite Brethren considered feetwashing an ordinance instituted by Christ to be practiced by
the church in a symbolic way immediately after the Lord's
Supper and in a practical way in daily life. Over a period of
years this symbolic reenactment has been phased out of most
congregational observances of the Lord's Supper, and the emphasis placed on its practical application. You can tell us how
well we do that. We invite you to help our society see that
miracle of love and be attracted to the One who showed us how.

7
Making peace
with peace

If you took the time to read the *Confession of Faith* of the
Mennonite Brethren, you would find that it has always included a section on "Love and Nonresistance." It's a belief that
produces many questions on the part of some members, particularly pertaining to the support of militarism in peacetime
and active involvement in wartime. Some think this doctrine
should attract searchers for truth as honey draws bees; others,
although fellow-heirs to this doctrine, are not ready to accept
this gift as gladly or as gratefully. They don't think it quite
belongs, and that it detracts from the real mission of the
church: evangelism and missions. Furthermore, they have the
perception, probably an accurate one at certain periods in our
history, that it's a doctrine we only get serious about during
wartime and then set aside when international peace has been
declared, making it seem as if the teachings of the Bible about
peace are not universally applicable when bombs and bullets
aren't flying.

Wesley J. Prieb, director of the Center for Mennonite Brethren Studies in Hillsboro, Kan., writes that we Mennonite Brethren, admittedly edgy about this principle, mute our peace witness because we use weak labels like "nonresistance" and "conscientious objector" which have a connotation of passivity to refer to a very strong and virile teaching. The biblical principle of love is both positive and active and entails "bearing the cross, servanthood, suffering love and overcoming love." Christian love is nonviolent, but never passive. Wartime resistance, traditionally the most dramatic and intense contrast of the way of violence with the way of love, is only one aspect of this doctrine. Which introduces the matter of the Christian's duty to the state, so let's say something about that first.

Mennonite Brethren generally see the state as part of God's arrangement for society to maintain order. The Christian has a responsibility to submit, support, honor and pray for leaders of government. But to what degree? What are we willing to be besides good citizens? What is the second mile here? Our answer would be that no form of government is "Christian." Government in all forms, whether tyrannical or democratic, communist or western, belongs to the "principalities and powers" the Apostle Paul writes about in Ephesians 6:12.

Theologian John E. Toews of the Mennonite Brethren Biblical Seminary writes that Romans 13 asks us to discriminate in our assessment of any form of government. We must ask: "Does the government govern justly in terms of rewarding good and evil according to the merits of each? Does the government demand more of us than we can rightly give?" Where there is a contradiction in the demands of government and the demands of God, the Christian's responsibility is to disobey the government and obey God.

The traditional Mennonite attitude toward state and government was separationist and apolitical: No participation in the police force. No voting. No running for government office. According to theologian Abe Dueck, this attitude is expressed in the Schleitheim Confession of 1527, which speaks of two orders, "one inside the perfection of Christ and the other outside the perfection of Christ." The state exists for the world to keep evil in check by means of coercion and violence. Christians cannot be involved in such action, and so they are to cooperate within the state only to the extent that such obedience to authorities does not conflict with their commitment to God; otherwise, they "should suffer quietly or seek to escape."

Early Mennonite Brethren in North America resolved not to become involved in political institutions, although there was some involvement at the local community level in school boards and town councils. Since World War 2, rapid change in attitude and practice of Mennonite Brethren regarding political involvement has occurred. From an earlier acceptance that government is necessary but not the responsibility of Christians, attitudes now include involvement, even in high levels of government, as both good and acceptable because of the social implications of the gospel. The traditional withdrawal position still exists, however, especially among older people. You will find Mennonite Brethren generally politically conservative, more ready to influence government from the outside than from the inside as an active participant in the political process.

The following peace statement appears in the *Confession of Faith*: "We believe that Christians should live by the law of love and practice the forgiveness of enemies as taught and exemplified by the Lord Jesus. The church as the body of Christ is a fellowship of redeemed, separated people, controlled by redemptive love. Its evangelistic responsibility is to present Christ, the Prince of Peace, as the answer to human need, enmity and violence. The evil, brutal and inhuman nature of war stands in contradiction to the new nature of the Christian.

"The Christian seeks to practice Christ's law of love in all relationships, and in all situations, including those involving personal injustice, social upheaval and international tensions. We believe that it is not God's will that Christians take up arms in military service but that, where possible, they perform alternate service to reduce strife, alleviate suffering and bear witness to the love of Christ" (Ex. 20:1-17; Mt. 5:17-28, 38-45; Rom. 12:19-21; 13:8-10; 1 Pet. 2:19-23).

The term "nonresistance" comes from Jesus's words in Matthew 5:39: "But I tell you, Do not resist an evil person. If someone strikes you on the right cheek, turn to him the other also" (*NIV*). In other words, don't pay back in like coin. Don't

return violence with more violence, but instead respond with
the nature of Jesus Christ, which is love. The basis of all our responses in peacetime or war is the new nature we receive in
Christ Jesus when we become believers. "The love of God is
shed abroad in our hearts." We can't return love for hate without this new nature, which makes peacemaking a way of life, a
conviction, not an ill-fitting coat we put on from time to time
when rumors of war appear.

The responsibility of a modern peacemaker includes the
following: (a) Prayer for enemies (Mt. 5:44) and for government
as well as all leaders (1 Tim. 2:8). Prayer is the first line of
offense. Every time we are given a spirit of discernment to see
faults or shortcomings in another person or group, it's time for
prayer, not for criticism or gossip. (b) Good deeds. Christ admonished his disciples to do good to them who hated them (Mt.
5:38-44). Love works no hardship on another person. The
church, as the body of Christ, provides the structure whereby
young and old can become part of this well-doing. Because
human life, anyone's life, is sacred to God, the Christian has
no right to help destroy it. His or her duty is to save life,
physically, spiritually and emotionally. Since the church's responsibility is to represent Christ, its head, and to spread the
gospel throughout the world, participation in violent action in
any form — personal or corporate, related to natural disaster
or to problems created because of human failings, such as family or intergenerational conflict, racial, sexual or social discrimination — should be out of the question for its members.

Young men and women are encouraged to live lives consistent with the scriptural and historic testimony of the Mennonite Brethren on peace. They are challenged to accept the government provision of alternative service, realizing that this
service offers a full expression of our objection to war. Mennonite Brethren are not ready to become political activists on
behalf of these teachings, nor to make Christ's words on peace
(Sermon on the Mount) normative for all believers, yet most
agree that we need clearer and stronger strategies for
peacemaking compatible with our desire to evangelize and
help in the formation of new congregations.

Closely related to the issues of love and peace are the matters of honesty and the oath. Our attitude toward these issues

often determines the difference between a "salty" Christian who affects his or her environment, and a flavorless one, who in the words of Jesus is "good-for-nothing, but to be cast out, and to be trodden underfoot of men."

Honesty reaches deep into a person's life. All Mennonites used to have a widespread reputation as a people who spoke the truth, a reputation that came with them from Europe. The word of Mennonites was as good as their bond. They believed as a body that honest people did not need to swear an oath in legal matters (Mt. 5:33-37; Jas. 5:12). In the early anabaptist writings, the non-swearing of the oath in a court of law was usually linked with the teaching of love and nonresistance. When Michael Sattler, one of the early European leaders, stood trial for the heresy of anabaptism, one of the charges against him was refusing to swear before authorities. He defended his

Michael Sattler stood trial for the heresy of anabaptism and was condemned to a martyr's death by burning. . . .

position on the basis of Matthew 5:34, but he was condemned to a martyr's death by burning.

Mennonites, including Mennonite Brethren, reject the implication of dishonesty resident in the oath, and therefore affirm the truth in legal transactions. "Oaths are of little use; good men do not need them, bad ones do not heed them." An oath pledges support of matters over which one has no control and is powerless to change. Also, the oath implies a double standard that all other statements not made under oath are untruthful, or might be untruthful, and only those made under oath can be believed.

The non-swearing of the oath was a main plank in the statement of faith in the early Mennonite church fathers. Jesus said, "I am the way, the truth and the life. No one comes to the Father but by me." Jesus embodied truth in human form. An absolute standard of truth was important to the early church with no room for white lies or small deceits. Today, heredity, environment or other persons take the blame for human failures, and this emphasis has gradually receded into the background of Mennonite teaching so that some newer converts rarely know its former strength. Honesty is still important with Christians, and with Mennonites, but it is no longer stated as a distinctive.

FOR ADDITIONAL READING:

Toews, J.A. *True Nonresistance Through Christ: A Study of Biblical Principles.* Hillsboro, Kan.: Board of Christian Literature, 1982.

Wenger, J.C. *The Way of Peace.* Scottdale, Pa.: Herald Press, n.d.

Drescher, John M. *Why I am a Conscientious Objector.* Scottdale, Pa.: Herald Press, 1982.

8
Far away and long ago:
The early history

It was a toss-up whether to start with where the Mennonite Brethren came from or with what we believe. It's sort of a version of the old chicken and egg argument. Now that I've told you quite a bit about us, I want to dig into history briefly to explain how the circumstances of history have molded us so that we emphasize certain aspects of biblical teaching and who some of the main personalities in this interesting historical drama were who are still influential today.

Our history as Mennonite Brethren had several stages. The first stage took place in Europe, the second in Prussia, the third in Russia, and the fourth in the United States and Canada and many other countries of the world. And we hope there'll be many more stages in the pilgrimage of this group as our witness spreads.

As I told you, Mennonites were named after the former priest, Menno Simons, but Menno wasn't the originator of the movement. Go back in time with me to the early decades of the 16th century. Like Dickens's *Tale of Two Cities*, it was the best of times, it was the worst of times. In western Europe the modern world was emerging. Like a long-slumbering giant still heavy with sleep, the people wrenched themselves loose from the past, heavily overgrown with traditionalism, and stumbled toward freedom in many areas, including religious freedom.

Feudalism, with its barbaric system of serfs and lords, had lost its grip on the land. Poverty, long-admired as a virtue of the saints, had become a social evil. The people had learned the worth of having enough to fill their stomachs and a little more.

Christopher Columbus had discovered America. Vasco da Gama had found a better trade route to India by sailing around Africa. The renaissance of art and science had peaked, but its influence continued. Gutenberg's invention of movable type had ushered in a new era of reading and learning. People were reading the Scriptures, not only in the original language but also in their own languages, and examining them against the backdrop of church teaching.

But the giant was not yet disencumbered of all old restraints. The people remained under heavy servitude to the state church — a fat, powerful institution with the pope as its sole sovereign. His local agents, the parish priests, achieved control of the populace by dispensing salvation like gumballs from a penny machine.

But people were beginning to think. They were becoming skeptical of traditional religious practices, such as the mass and pilgrimages, of the promised supernatural power of the relics of saints, and of the redemptive value of indulgences (spiritual favors sold for money). Around supper tables, in sheltered corners, at the marketplace and behind the carpenter's bench, church practices were being questioned. How could money-greedy, immoral priests be the keepers of the eternal souls of the people?

The struggle was alive in other arenas as well. In England, Henry VIII of the many wives was playing his games with the pope for his own reasons. In Europe, the astronomer Copernicus had declared openly in direct opposition to the teachings of the Roman Catholic Church that the earth rotated on its axis and that the earth and planets revolved around the sun. Even churchmen doubted the doctrines they preached.

And so the state church, the invincible Gibraltar for long centuries, was cracking at the foundation. But not without a struggle, for power relishes more power.

After the monk Martin Luther had made one of the first serious assaults on the church by nailing his ninety-five theses to the church door at Wittenberg, other individuals joined the struggle for a free church. The Reformation had begun, but much blood would be shed before freedom of belief was won for all.

In Switzerland, a twenty-seven-year-old university student confronted this power structure which was hiding the true light of the gospel from the people and recognized his life-task: This edifice must come down; people must be free to worship God as the Scriptures taught.

Conrad Grebel would hardly have been considered promising material for promoting a religious reformation before the spring of 1522. While at the university, he followed his friends' example to make life exciting. Drinking, brawling and loose living created more interesting activity than studying. During one fight he severely wounded his hand; another time, two Frenchmen were killed. Later in life he was plagued with an illness contracted because of his promiscuity. "Deservedly so," he wrote, "since I have often slept with women."

The generation gap was also Grebel's problem. He and his father, a wealthy Swiss businessman and influential civic leader, couldn't communicate. Money became a touchy issue.

After the monk Martin Luther nailed his ninety-five theses to the church door at Wittenberg, other individuals joined the struggle for a free church. . . .

The elder Grebel found his son's spendthrifty ways displeasing. The younger man blamed his father for not teaching him how to spend money wisely.

His parents didn't like his choice of future wife, a woman beneath his social class. Defiantly, he married her without their permission. His intelligence and bravado were matched at times only by his impudence. On one occasion, he wrote a former teacher who had admonished him, "Sniff onions and go hang."

In 1520 Grebel returned to his homeland without a degree, without a goal in life, frustrated and in disgrace. Shortly thereafter, he bumped into a group of students studying the Greek classics under Ulrich Zwingli, a teacher and pastor. He joined the group, and the teaching caught, especially the truths of the Scriptures. They made much sense to this life-weary student.

That spring at the end of a long trail of empty frustration, Grebel encountered the Christ of the Gospels. The exact date of his conversion is unknown, but by July of 1522 he was preaching the gospel publicly. He left behind the brawling lifestyle of the contemporary university student and committed himself to becoming a disciple of Christ.

Among this youthful group of Zwingli followers were George Blaurock, so called because he wore a blue coat, and Felix Manz. They and others attached themselves to their teacher like barnacles to the hull of a ship. He seemed an excellent choice for a leader. Grebel and his new friends were overjoyed to be on the side of a man who recognized the corruption of the church and was unafraid to speak out against it. Zwingli preached against the superstition in the church. He decried the idleness of the priests and their gluttony, drinking and immorality. He insisted on repentance and a change of life for the believer. Yes, Zwingli made lots of sense to these young idealists.

Grebel had enjoyed swinging his fists for trivial causes; now he thrilled to the excitement of fighting without fists for a much greater purpose ... and knowing he had God on his side.

This small group of reformers were intent on putting right in their lifetime the sins which had developed in the church over several centuries. Grebel, Blaurock and Manz began their struggle by preaching from the pulpits of the churches against the monks. The civic leaders, upset by these upstarts who were creating unrest among the people, forbade such preaching.

The young reformers tried other tactics. At a church parade, one of their group defiantly carried an open Bible instead of the customary relics of dead saints, saying, "This is the true, sacred thing; the others are only dead men's bones." He got his knuckles rapped for mocking the symbols of official Christendom.

The struggle continued. At their frequent and intensive

Bible studies these "brethren" produced a new plan for the church of Jesus Christ patterned after New Testament principles, freeing the people from the domination of the priests.

The group came to Zwingli with their plan for the church, which in particular asked for the abolishment of the mass, the main papal ceremony and the central means of controlling the people. They saw the mass and the use of images in the church as a direct violation of the Word of God. They expected Zwingli to agree, but he hesitated. The time was not ripe for reform before the people were ready for it, he insisted.

Though Zwingli was a church reformer, he was not ready to sacrifice his influence over the wealthy Zurich citizens for a quick change. He sensed the city council was not yet ready to get rid of the mass, and he feared a church schism. He couldn't see how Grebel's model of the church and the present form could exist side by side under state control. Like young puppies nipping at the heels of their master, the young men forced Zwingli to face the issues. They were developing and insisting upon the very principles he had taught them. Yet with each new request for reform, he shoved them aside.

Their conflict moved into the open with a public debate, particularly concerning the abolishment of the mass and the use of images. The Grebel group considered these an abomination of Satan. After a lengthy open discussion, it became apparent to Grebel no decision would be made to get rid of these practices, so he requested that the debate be continued the next day.

Zwingli, who continued to accept that the civic government had the authority to decide all matters regarding church practice, replied curtly to his erstwhile followers: "The council will decide whatever regulations are to be adopted in the future regarding the mass." At once a follower of Grebel sprang to his feet, "Mr. Ulrich, you do not have the right to place the matter of the decision regarding the mass in the hands of the council, for the decision has already been made. The Spirit of God has decided." With this, the rift between Zwingli and his former disciples became a gaping chasm.

The next issue to widen the breach even more was infant baptism. In the Catholic Church, infants were baptized or christened (made Christian) at birth without their knowledge or consent. Zwingli had earlier in his career preached against infant baptism as being unscriptural. He had convinced Grebel and his friends of the unreasonableness of this practice. Now he changed his view and stated that the best interests of the church required infant baptism.

His vacillation was hard to understand and to bear, for Grebel had come to see that a Christian was one who had personally accepted Christ and had committed his life to following him. Baptism and admission into the church should follow conversion, not precede it. Being a Christ-follower required an adult commitment. He could not accept infant baptism again.

This issue, like the matter of the mass and images, was debated hotly. On August 11, 1524, the city council demanded that all citizens have their children baptized at birth or pay a fine. The command held no power. Everywhere the common people disobeyed it. So the council issued a firmer decree demanding that all who failed to have their babies baptized by a priest within eight days after birth were to be exiled with wife, child and household effects. Zwingli, influential in leading the council, was determined this new movement must be crushed to maintain civil and ecclesiastical order. He also believed the "spirituals" would yield under such stringent measures. He was disappointed. The movement gained momentum with more and more parents refusing to have their babies baptized.

Another public debate was held on January 17, 1525. Three days later the principal leaders of the opposition to the state position were served notice to conform, get out of the country, or face imprisonment.

One chilly winter evening about a week after the debate, Grebel's group met as usual at the home of Felix Manz, near the Grossmuenster. After praying together, they each felt the presence of the Holy Spirit. With great fear, Blaurock stood up and asked Grebel for God's sake to baptize him with the true Christian baptism upon his faith. He knelt before the other young man, who then baptized him by sprinkling him with water. Then Blaurock baptized the others, and each ordained one another to the ministry of the gospel. The newly baptized group pledged themselves, as true disciples of Christ, to live separated from the world.

Believer's baptism, the baptism of accountable persons, had been introduced to the church. Anabaptism (to baptize again) was born and the free church movement begun. With this act the group cut themselves loose both from the Reformed movement of Christendom (of which Zwingli was the leader) and from Catholicism. The date was January 25, 1525.

Like a mammoth Roman candle which explodes into the air, suddenly illuminating the darkness, so the new teaching burst into life. Wherever a spark fell, a new candle was lit. Within three or four days the group had baptized fifteen persons. The anabaptists, as the group was derogatorily called, went from house to house witnessing to their new-found faith. Because of their evangelistic and missionary zeal, the movement grew among peasants and proletarians. In April of the same year, Grebel baptized a throng of new converts.

Zwingli didn't like it. He was forced to call for government help to squash this movement which had slipped the traces of state control. The believers were taunted with names, charged with all kinds of crimes, fined, exiled, imprisoned, tortured and finally executed by drowning or burning at the stake. Undaunted, the anabaptists continued to hold secret meetings at which they studied the Bible and looked for ways to reproduce the church of the Book of Acts in pure form.

Though hunted like wild animals, their only weapons were love and truth. Instead of carrying a sword as was common, they bore only a wooden stave in their belts. In their preaching they insisted that conversion must be the result of the conviction of a sinful life, that the church must be composed of regenerated professing believers, that the church and state must remain separate, and that good works must be the fruit of faith. Discipleship (suffering servanthood) must be based on love, not violence. They were willing to die that these truths might live.

The early leaders never saw the fruit of their efforts. Grebel died of the bubonic plague several years later. To show contempt for his crime, the authorities killed Manz by drowning, a form of execution usually reserved for women. Blaurock was exiled.

But the truth for which they gave their lives leaped to all

parts of Europe to become the radical left wing of the Reform movement. In Holland, a disgruntled Catholic priest, Menno Simons by name, became convinced of the truth of anabaptist teaching and accepted the leadership of this evangelical group in Holland and Germany, which became the first free church of modern church history — not part of a state-church system.

It's taken me a while to get to Menno Simons, after whom the Mennonites were named, but this background is important to understand what's coming next.

9
Far away and long ago: The founder

If you travel to the village of Witmarsum in Holland, near the North Sea, you will find a monument erected in an outlying area, somewhat hidden by trees, dedicated to the memory of Menno Simons, whose name has been attached to Mennonite denominations for over four hundred years. He provided leadership to the scattered and fragmented group of anabaptists, drawing them together doctrinally as he traveled among them. His voluminous writings helped to hold together the congregations often confronted by fanatics offering strange teachings.

Menno Simons (1496-1561) writes in his own biographical sketch that he entered the priesthood in his father's village of Pingjum, Friesland, in Holland, and fulfilled his duties like his colleagues — in a light-hearted manner, "gambling, drinking" and in similar empty amusements. He knew a little Greek and Latin, but admitted to knowing little about the Scriptures. He feared he would be led astray if he read the Bible, and so he spoke derisively about this book, if at all.

A chain of circumstances caused him to rethink his attitude toward the Scriptures. One day while distributing the elements at mass this carefree priest was troubled by the question whether the bread and wine were actually the Lord's flesh and some of Luther's writings, and became convinced the teaching of transubstantiation was a human invention. Yet he tion continued to trouble him, he studied the New Testament and some of Luther's writings, and became convinced the teaching of transubstantiation was a human invention. Yet he continued to preach in his parish.

About this time anabaptists appeared in the area. They were considered heretics and called by this name deliberately because it connected directly with the old Roman Empire practice of putting to death anyone who was baptized a second time. One of the anabaptists, a God-fearing pious man named Sicke Snyder, was beheaded at Leeuwarden because he had been rebaptized. Menno had never heard of anyone being baptized twice. Once again he was bothered by what he saw. What if the church was wrong on this score as it had been on the mass? He studied the Bible and could find no mention of infant baptism in it.

A third event had an even greater impact on him. A number of anabaptists called Muensterites appeared in the area. Though pious and zealous people, they had been led astray and were teaching strange doctrines related to polygamy and using force to set up an earthly kingdom. When they took up arms to defend themselves against opposing government forces and many were killed, Menno's brother among them, their deaths weighed heavily upon his heart. He wrote that with his own eyes he had seen those zealous people willingly sacrifice property and life for their convictions, although these convictions were in error. However, though he wanted to remain true to Christ, he wanted even more to live comfortably. He was not willing to lay down his life for his beliefs.

His misgivings about the discrepancies between the teachings of the Bible and the practice and doctrine taught by the Catholic Church caused him much inner turmoil. For about nine months he remained in the Catholic Church, preaching boldly about repentance, baptism and the Lord's Supper "according to the Spirit and doctrine of Christ." He warned against false teachings.

On Sunday, January 30, 1536, he was finally free to renounce his position, reputation, name, the doctrine of infant baptism and the easy life, and to submit to a life of stress and poverty "under the heavy cross of Christ" and identify with the anabaptists. No one knows exactly when Menno was rebaptized, nor where he lived for several years thereafter. He wrote in 1544 that he couldn't find a cabin or hut in which his wife and little children could live safely for as long as a year or even six months; an Imperial Decree had been issued against him, forbidding anyone to shelter him and offering a large reward for his capture. During about eighteen years of persecution and thereafter, until his death in 1561, he preached, baptized, wrote and ordained elders and organized the growing church.

Many stories have developed about his period of flight, of which he writes as a time which he had to "tolerate being called anabaptist, hedge-preacher, deceiver and heretic, and be greeted in the name of the devil." Once when fleeing from his pursuers, he was seated outside with the driver. When some soldiers stopped the coach, they asked the driver, "Is Menno Simons inside?" Menno turned around and called out, "Is Menno Simons in there?" The passengers said he wasn't. The soldiers, satisfied, went on. Another time, the story is told, a man who had agreed to betray Menno as he passed by in a boat became tongue-tied, and Menno escaped.

When some soldiers stopped the coach, they asked the driver, "Is Menno Simons inside?"

The term "Mennist" was first used by Countess Anna of East Friesland in 1544 to distinguish between the peaceful followers of Menno and the revolutionary and fanatical element among the anabaptists to help her decide who should be expelled from her kingdom. Menno's influence was so great that within a decade the name had stuck. Here, briefly stated, are some of Menno Simons's teachings which he promoted and to which Mennonite Brethren later turned in their search for truth:

1. The Bible is the sole authority in matters of faith and life. This authority does not reside in the state church.

2. The divine grace of God is needed for salvation.

3. All believers share the responsibility to spread the gospel.

4. Only believers should be baptized, followed by voluntary church membership.

5. The Lord's Supper should be instituted scripturally.

6. All believers should live holy lives in obedience to God's Word.

7. Believers should exhibit Christlike love for members of his body.

8. They should boldly confess Christ as the Son of God.

9. They should willingly suffer oppression and tribulation for the sake of the Lord's Word in a nonresistant way.

10. The church and state should function as separate entities.

Menno Simons placed 1 Corinthians 3:11 on the title page of all his writings, indicating he believed that obedience to Christ was central to the Christian life: "For no one can lay any foundation other than the one already laid, which is Jesus Christ" (*NIV*).

As a result of severe persecutions of the anabaptists in Switzerland and Holland thousands fled to other countries, particularly to Prussia, where their readiness to work hard was welcomed by the large estate owners who needed laborers to drain their swampy lowlands. The Mennonites established churches, built farms and windmills, planted orchards and gardens — and even became wealthy.

When Frederick William became king in 1786 the Mennonites' refusal to become involved in the war effort, the jealousy of neighbors of their successful farming, and government restrictions on the purchase of more land for their growing families, forced them to look for a new home. Catherine the Great of Russia was looking for industrious settlers for new territories acquired north of the Black Sea and invited the Mennonites to her land, promising them generous privileges related to freedom of faith, nonparticipation in the military, land ownership and the right to govern their own colonies. The Mennonites accepted the invitation. In 1787 the first Mennonite immigrants, mostly poor and uneducated families, arrived at their destination in south Russia to be followed shortly by many others in large contingents over the next few years.

Although the first years were extremely difficult on the barren steppes of the Ukraine, the immigrants were determined to succeed. Again they planted crops and orchards, built homes, church buildings and schools, and generally prospered in numbers. By 1860 the Mennonite population in Russia increased to about 30,000 persons, living in small villages of about twenty to thirty families each, with almost complete autonomy in educational, religious, economic and civic affairs. Because of the lack of strong leadership, however, spiritual life was at a low ebb. Here and there individuals longed for greater spiritual vitality.

FOR ADDITIONAL READING:

Simons, Menno. *The Complete Writings of Menno Simons*. Translated from the Dutch by Leonard Verduin and edited by John C. Wenger. Scottdale, Pa.: Herald Press, 1956.

Dyck, Cornelius J., ed. *An Introduction to Mennonite History*. Scottdale, Pa., 1967.

Bender, Harold S. and John Horsch. *Menno Simons' Life and Writings: A Quadricentennial Tribute, 1536-1936*. Hesston, Kan.: Gospel Publishers, 1970.

Wenger, J.C. *How the Mennonites Came to Be*. Scottdale, Pa.: Herald Press, 1977.

10
Far away and long ago:
The Russian interlude

If a former Catholic priest was the first reformer of the
Mennonites, the second reformer for the Mennonite Brethren
was a Lutheran pastor. Menno Simons built the foundation,
but Pastor Eduard Wuest, already mentioned several times,
contributed the most to the spirit of the Mennonite Brethren
Church before its official organization. But even his name is
not one you may hear as much today as some later leaders.

Eduard Hugo Otto Wuest came to Russia in 1845 at age
28 after being ousted from his parish in Germany because of
a colleague's jealousy of his success as a congregational leader.
The previous year he had experienced a spiritual rebirth and
had begun to relate to pietists, such as the Moravian Brethren
and Methodists. Wuest, a handsome man with a charismatic

personality, drew a large following. Mennonites already interested in the pietistic movement attended his installation
services at Neuhoffnung near the sea of Azov and then followed
his ministry closely.

A fiery preacher, Wuest emphasized the free grace of God
for salvation, the need of a consciousness of sin, Christ-like
love for one another and, particularly, a more vital religious
experience. He directed his listeners away from "the emptiness
and despair of their own hearts to the fullness of divine mercy."
Revival broke out. But here, as in Germany, he incurred the
wrath of the elders and ministers of both the Lutheran and
Mennonite congregations who didn't want his influence in
their flocks and forbade him to preach in their meeting places
or in homes.

Among the Mennonites were those who wanted to hear
more from this man who stressed spontaneity of worship and
the glorious freedom of spirit the gospel produced. They were
weary of the lifeless formal services with their dearth of
spiritual nourishment. They invited Wuest to their homes on
Saturday afternoons. After someone else had preached to a
gathering of interested persons, they asked him to answer
questions about the Scriptures. These people who met in this
fashion called each other "brother" and "sister" to reflect their
close spiritual relationship.

A clash between Wuest and his followers and the established Mennonite church leaders was inevitable. But he died
in 1859 at the age of 42 before the spiritual liberation movement he had started could coalesce into a strong body. Unlike
Menno, he was not the leader to teach consistent doctrine and
draw the people together.

Wuest's death meant the converts among the Mennonites
during his five-year ministry had to find another way to flesh
out their new understanding of Scripture, the Christian life
and the church. In the village of Gnadenfeld, which had been
the center of the revival, some of these "brethren" and "sisters"
gathered regularly for Bible teaching and prayer. Out of their
reaction to taking communion in the mother church with
people who made no open profession of salvation, they asked a
church elder who was somewhat sympathetic to their cause to
serve the Lord's Supper more often and at times other than

those set by the church calendar. He refused. Private communion had no historical precedent in the Mennonite church. Other elders couldn't see why young and healthy men and women couldn't come to the regular service for this ordinance like the others; the leaders only conducted communion in a home to accommodate the sick and elderly.

Discouraged at the refusal of their request, a small group of believers from several congregations met in late November of 1859 in a home to observe this ordinance without the sanction of the elders. The outcome was as expected. At a hearing before the church elders, the six members of the Gnadenfeld church who had participated in the Lord's Supper were persuaded to promise that "they would submit to all things not contrary to the Word of God and their conscience."

Attempts at reconciliation between the two groups would have been successful if it had not been for the fact that at the next meeting a few members of the new group, derisively referred to as the "saints" and "brethren," were vocally attacked by a group of critics. Some members shouted, "Out with them; they are no better than the others (the ones who had participated in the Lord's Supper)." The critics threatened to turn the "brethren" over to the civil authorities if they did not desist from their practices. At that, one of the brethren, Jacob Reimer, approached the elder in charge and asked for permission to leave. The more vocal opposition members called out, "Why don't you allow them to leave?"

Sorrowfully, the elder, whose sympathies were somewhat with the group, said, "Well, then, brethren, leave!" But when it seemed as if only Reimer and Johann Claassen were moving toward the door, someone called to Claassen, "As a rule you are a courageous man, so call on your friends to go with you!" Claassen turned around to say, "Well, brothers?" About ten men walked out of the church. Altogether the Gnadenfeld congregation lost about twenty-five members as a result of this departure to start a house movement, the outcome of which few foresaw at the time.

On January 6, 1860, eighteen family heads signed a hurriedly composed document of secession from the mother church, which they referred to as the *Kirchliche* (churchy or ecclesiastical body). On January 18 nine other family heads from

Sorrowfully, the elder, whose sympathies were somewhat with the group, said, "Well, then, brethren, leave!"

other congregations added their names. This charter membership of the Mennonite Brethren Church consisted, therefore, of
over fifty people, for each signature usually signified a man
and wife.

The result of that step was a tense struggle between the
mother church and the secessionists reaching into all areas of
life: social, economic, political, educational and religious. The
conflict lasted until 1866 when the new group received legal
recognition by the Russian government as a Mennonite congregation with full privileges under the original charter by which
Empress Catherine had allowed the Mennonites into Russia.
This struggle had many of the same overtones which the struggle between the state church and anabaptists had three
hundred years earlier, for it also became a civic issue. The
local church and civic leaders saw these young men and their
wives as hotheaded, thick-skulled zealots who considered
themselves the only ones able to interpret the will of God, and
therefore used their legal powers to deny them their civic
rights to carry on business and so forth.

The secession documents speak to the reasons the "brethren" were seceding. The issues were not primarily doctrinal, but had to do with leadership, church practices and ethical issues, as has frequently been the case when schisms have occurred in the Mennonite family. The brethren deplored the lack of emphasis on the need for personal conversion before becoming a church member. At that time anyone born into a Mennonite family could become a church member and partake of the Lord's Supper. The document also spoke to the issue that baptism was being administered to anyone who asked for it, as long as he or she was of Mennonite birth.

The documents deplored the morals of the people, their excessive drinking at weddings and hog butcherings, the cold, formal services, and the apathetic leadership. The new group asked to be recognized as a separate congregation within the Mennonite body. They did not want to leave the Mennonite fold. To support their thinking on this latter matter, the secessionists frequently quoted Scripture, but also Menno Simons. They agreed with the anabaptists on the separation of church and state, rejection of war and taking up of arms, sharing of goods, and the baptism of adult believers as opposed to infants. They knew that if they did not gain legal recognition as a Mennonite body, they would lose all civic rights under the Russian government, a disastrous outcome. Historian Henry Krahn states: "They did not want to be Pietistic, nor Baptist, but rather Mennonite. They wanted to be and remain historical and consistent Mennonitism, a pure Mennonitism that was based not upon birth, but upon rebirth."

The church elders refused to recognize them as a Mennonite church and banned (excommunicated) the group, which meant they had to go to the Russian government for legal recognition. In the meantime, they faced imprisonment, exile, corporal punishment, social and economic ostracism, and the constant threat of loss of civic privileges at the hands of their own compatriots. The grim story of this battle between the two factions is not pleasant, but once the secessionists had decided to pull out, there was no compromise for them.

Historians state that some of the brethren's accusations against the Mennonite church in Russia were possibly too severe, for the revival begun at Gnadenfeld flourished thereafter and some congregations grew spiritually. Had the brethren been a little more patient, they might have gained their goals without a schism. Their secession landed them later on into other problems for which they were not prepared: excessive emotionalism and too literal Bible interpretation.

In the meantime, the brethren held meetings in homes until they could build a meeting place; they appointed elders and baptized believers, and finally received official recognition from the Russian government as a Mennonite church. The first years were beset by ups and downs, with periods of fanaticism on the part of some, developing Wuest's emphasis on an uninhibited and demonstrative practice of worship. At the same time, other emphases grew stronger: conversion should be based on the grace of God for forgiveness. It should be a definite experience, a turning, not merely a natural process heightened by catechism. It should reveal by a change in the person's life a movement away from sin and worldliness. Baptism should be by immersion (not sprinkling) upon confession of faith to symbolize the death and resurrection of Christ. Communion would be held frequently, followed by feetwashing. They acknowledged the need to proclaim the Good News openly and boldly.

A strong spirit of evangelism and missions developed not only for the immediate neighborhood but also for peoples in other lands. At times, some of the brethren invited themselves to homes of the *Kirchliche* (churchly Mennonites) to enlighten them, which was sometimes interpreted as arrogance, sometimes as evangelism. But despite human failings, the group grew, and by 1872 had about 600 members and the beginnings of a strong mission program abroad.

FOR ADDITIONAL READING:

Bekker, Jacob P. *Origin of the Mennonite Brethren Church.* Tr.
     by D.E. Pauls and A.E. Janzen, Hillsboro, Kan.: The Menno-
     nite Brethren Historical Society of the Midwest, 1973.

Friesen, P.M. *The Mennonite Brotherhood in Russia (1789-1910).*
     Tr. by J.B. Toews, Abraham Friesen, Peter J. Klassen and Harry
     Loewen. Winnipeg, Man.: Board of Christian Literature, 1978.

Klassen, Elizabeth Suderman. *Trailblazer for the Brethren.*
     Scottdale, Pa.: Herald Press, 1978.

Toews, J.A. *A History of the Mennonite Brethren Church*. Hillsboro, Kan.: Board of Christian Literature, 1975.

Wiebe, David V. *They Seek a Country*. Hillsboro, Kan.: published by author, 1959.

Wiebe, David V. *Grace Meadow: The Story of Gnadenau and Its First Elder*. Hillsboro, Kan.: Mennonite Brethren Publishing House, 1967.

Wiebe, Katie Funk. *Women Among the Brethren*. Hillsboro, Kan.: Board of Christian Literature, 1979.

11
The church expanding

One of the unique traits of Mennonite Brethren is their zeal for missions. When the first group organized, they immediately started thinking of evangelizing others and passing on the good news of the gospel. That spirit has stayed with our congregations to the present. When the Mennonite Brethren congregations in three settlements in Russia gathered for the first General Conference in 1872, twelve years after their founding, the original group of eighteen families had expanded to 600 members. By 1925 40 percent of the Mennonite population of the daughter colonies and 15.5 percent of the other colonies had joined this movement.

But at the same time, Mennonites, including Mennonite Brethren, were steadily migrating to other countries, particularly the United States. The Czarist government was pressuring its colonists, including the Mennonites, to become more like the Russians in language and culture. On the other hand, land for settlement for the increasing Mennonite population was decreasing. The Mennonites had entered Russia with a pledge from the government that they would be exempt from military service; that promise now looked as if it wouldn't hold with increasing demands upon the Mennonites to serve in the armed forces.

What to do? Mennonites sold land, buildings, homes and equipment cheaply; and slowly but steadily, beginning in 1874, left for the land of promise — America. About 10,000 settled in Kansas, Nebraska, Minnesota and the Dakotas in the United States in the next decade; and about 8,000 settled primarily in the East and West Reserves of Manitoba in Canada. Among the new settlers was a group of about thirty-five families known as the Krimmer Mennonite Brethren (because they lived in the Crimea) who had also seceded from the mother church in Russia about 1867 under the leadership of Elder Jacob A. Wiebe. Few Mennonite Brethren joined the

Mennonites, including Mennonite Brethren, were steadily migrating to other countries, particularly the United States. . . .

Canadian immigrants (most of which were from the conservative groups), but many joined those headed for the United
States. Members of the Mennonite Church (formerly Old Mennonites) helped in both countries to get the Russian-Menno-
nites settled in their new home.

According to historian J.A. Toews, the early period in
North America (1874-79) was characterized by religious fer-
ment and inner tensions. Settlers from different colonies in
Russia could not agree in their new homeland on church practices, like mode of baptism. The sorting into groups and congregations continued for several years. By 1878, the first gathering of Mennonite Brethren Church representatives was held
near Henderson, Nebraska, with eleven people present to discuss common interests, chief of which has remained a continu-
ing concern: how to unite all Mennonite Brethren congregations into one strong body so that they can fulfill the mandate
of Christ to spread the gospel to all nations. The early conferences were marked by a keen interest in missions and
evangelism. They also discussed how to continue the work of
missions begun in Russia as well as how to order their corporate lives to the greatest glory of God. Early issues which seem
less significant today were the "sister-kiss," head coverings for
women, positions in government, excommunication, form of
baptism, and intermarriage with persons of other confessions.
Itinerant preachers were regularly appointed to serve widely
scattered congregations and members.

Expansion went forward rapidly after the first congregations had formed: into Manitoba and Saskatchewan in the
1890s and thereafter; into Colorado in the late 1880s; into Oklahoma when these Indian territories were opened up for settlement in the 1890s; into Texas before World War 1; and into
California, Oregon and Washington after the turn of the century.

A small black conference of six congregations, located in
North Carolina, came into the Mennonite Brethren fold in 1960
through the merger of the Krimmer Mennonite Brethren with
the MBs. Merger with this church body, similar to the Mennonite Brethren in many aspects but with a stronger social conscience, had been considered before without success. However,
as the result of inter-church fellowship and a good working

relationship in several areas over a period of years, the two bodies joined to become one conference. The KMB mission program became part of the MB effort. The Latin America Mennonite Brethren Conference (LAMB) in South Texas, which began as a mission outreach, has about a half-dozen Spanish congregations. A number of Hispanic churches are also flourishing in California.

Mennonites have come to Canada in a number of "waves," the first to Ontario from Eastern Pennsylvania. The second wave has already been referred to when large numbers settled in southern Manitoba. The largest group arrived during the 1920s, following World War 1 and the Russian Revolution, with about 20,000 finding homes primarily in the prairie provinces. A fourth wave came after World War 2 directly from Europe and later from South America. Each wave brought with it Mennonite Brethren adherents.

Canadian Mennonite Brethren began at Burwalde near Winkler, Manitoba, with the formation of the first church in 1886. The gathering of Mennonite Brethren in General Confer-

Mennonites found their way to Alberta when "one man and his family decided to clean sugar beets for a local farmer."

ence sessions took place at the Winkler church in 1898 in an enlarged structure. Mennonites were also attracted to Saskatchewan because free homesteads and cheap land were available. Mennonite Brethren, together with other Mennonites, settled in the northern area near Rosthern first and then also around Herbert. Mennonites found their way to Alberta, one writer states, when "one man and his family decided to clean sugar beets for a local farmer" in the fall of 1925. He and his family were followed by a stream of others looking for a better home, Mennonite Brethren among them.

In the ten years from 1925 on, thirteen new churches were formed in Alberta and British Columbia, where only one had existed briefly before. Activity in Ontario was apparent in 1925 with the formation of the first Mennonite Brethren congregation in the Kitchener-Waterloo area. As Mennonite Brethren became more aware of the needs of others, and because of the unsettled conditions in the Congo, MB missionaries who could speak French began an evangelistic and church planting ministry in Quebec in 1960. That work has grown so that today twelve (including one English church) are thriving, and their leaders look toward expanding their witness to many more among the French-speaking people of Quebec in the next decade. "Nowhere in all of the North American Mennonite Brethren is there likely as zealous a band of evangelists as among the French-Canadian Quebec churches," writes the Canadian MB journalist Harold Jantz. The long range goal is to also have an Atlantic Mennonite Brethren Conference of churches ready for Canadian affiliation within fifteen years.

But the movement hasn't stopped there. Vigorous church growth is also evident in the northern areas of Manitoba, Alberta and British Columbia. In Vancouver, Chinese, Greek and East Indian churches are developing. "Church planting is the most effective way of evangelism," says Canadian minister James Nikkel. "We could have evangelistic crusades, but they don't have the same effect."

For many years, the largest Mennonite Brethren population was in the United States, but gradually the Canadian churches have outstripped the U.S. In 1983, the Canadian churches included 23,500 members in 170 churches. The

United States churches numbered 17,000 members in 125 churches.

Church growth has become a major concern of U.S. and Canadian Mennonite Brethren in the last decades. Mennonite Brethren, like many other people, have flocked to the economic opportunities of the West Coast and the large cities. Congregations which have grown most quickly have been those where a nucleus of Mennonite Brethren already live and to whom others can be added from the unchurched and also from other denominations. Growth in all geographic areas has not always been as much as expected, planned or desired.

Up to 1909, the General Conference met annually, but soon the long distances some delegates had to travel led to the formation of district conferences meeting annually. The result was the Southern, Central and Pacific Districts, the LAMB Conference, and the North Carolina Conference in the United States and six provincial conferences in Canada. The General Conference, which meets triennially, gathered for its 56th convention in 1984 in Reedley, Calif., where it celebrated the centennial of its overseas missions efforts. The site of the sessions alternates between Canada and the United States.

So what does all this detail mean? Not that the task of evangelizing is done, but that if we continue faithful and obedient to God's calling, he will continue to add to his church and bring glory to his name.

12
Growth through missions and evangelism

Consider for a moment what a hundred dollars can buy: a video game, an evening's entertainment for a small group of friends or maybe even a bicycle for a youngster. In 1884 Mennonite Brethren congregations in America pledged $100 annually to support a national worker serving with the American Baptists in India, for they had no work of their own. The first offering toward this goal was $26.36.

In 1984, a hundred years later, Mennonite Brethren congregations are supporting about 150 missionaries, fourteen Christian Service workers and twelve Good News Corps workers, in addition to numerous national pastors, teachers and other kinds of workers in countries of every major continent. The budget of the Board of Missions and Services today exceeds five million dollars. Mennonite Brethren in overseas countries far outnumber those of us who live in North America where the organized and sending churches are located. A deep-rooted concern and wholehearted enthusiasm for missions coupled with prayer and effort caused that hundred-dollar seed to grow to such vast proportions.

Actually the spark for missions was ignited earlier in southern Russia. Government restrictions on proselytizing members of the Russian Orthodox Church hindered evangelism for the young church, so its members looked elsewhere. Abram and Maria Friesen of the Molotschna colony opened a field in India in 1889 under the American Baptist Mission Union with Mennonite Brethren support; seven years later the church there was blessed with seven hundred converts to the Christian faith. Other missionaries followed to India soon thereafter.

North American support for that first national worker in India was extended to six persons, then to the Cameroons in Africa. Peter H. and Martha Wedel and Henry and Maria Enns joined the Baptists in the Cameroons in Africa in 1896. The Mennonite Brethren mission program was launched. Missionaries were commissioned to bring the gospel message to nationals of other lands with the full blessing and support of the home congregations; they later returned to tell the home constituency at mission festivals and other services the great things that were happening overseas. Mission prayer circles sprang up in congregations, forming the basis for most women's missionary circles functioning today. Prayer bands were formed in church schools. Everyone wanted a part,

Everyone wanted a part, whether it was providing funds, prayer support, items to complete the outfit of the outgoing missionary or to donate clothing and bedding for the poor. . . .

whether it was to provide funds, prayer support, items to complete the outfit of the outgoing missionary or to donate clothing and bedding for the poor of another country. Contributing to other mission programs was no longer sufficient for these congregations; within a matter of years Mennonite Brethren had developed programs in Oklahoma, India, China, Congo (now Zaire) and Paraguay.

Journalist Harold Jantz writes that one of the characteristics of Mennonite Brethren missions has been for forward-looking individuals and small mission societies to lead the way into new areas, whereupon the church has followed with funds and personnel. Mennonite Brethren moved into China, the Congo (later Zaire) through two organizations, into Paraguay with the help of Mennonites there, and into Colombia through the interest of a mission-minded group in northern Saskatchewan. World War 2 temporarily halted the overseas missions activity, but at the end of the war the conference made a major movement ahead into Africa, Latin America, Colombia, Japan, Ecuador (radio ministry) and Europe, and workers are helping under other agencies in Nepal, Afghanistan and Bangladesh.

You will frequently hear of BOMAS or Missions/Services, an acronym for the Board of Missions and Services, which carries responsibility for all decisions related to the total mission effort. Missionaries carry responsibility for the method of work, pattern of program and standard of accomplishment. The goal of all involved is to build indigenous churches that will evangelize their communities for Jesus Christ. The priorities of the mission program are church planting and evangelism, followed by leadership recruitment and development and nurture of young churches. Vernon Wiebe, former missions general secretary, says the task is "to tell the good news, form indigenous fellowships, help people in need by working creatively where we are pioneers, working cooperatively where the church exists, working noninstitutionally wherever possible; establishing Mennonite Brethren churches where possible; helping other churches and/or agencies to establish believers' churches; working as models and as expert resources to the work, ministering to human need."

BOMAS directs this goal through various means: All kinds of evangelism — friendship, home Bible studies, media ministries, literature ministries, large ministries; through teaching at Bible institutes and seminaries operated by indigenous Mennonite Brethren conferences and in training programs of other missions; through literacy training, vocational training centers, development work, agricultural projects; through medical missions, education, preaching and pastoral work; and through media ministries such as radio broadcasting.

Radio broadcasting is an important aspect of evangelism. For thirty years BOMAS has helped staff the German department of HCJB, Quito, Ecuador, which releases a dozen regular broadcasts daily, with about two thirds of responses coming from Europe. In India, BOMAS and Trans World Radio sponsor a Telugu language radio and literature ministry. Two weekly Russian broadcasts, produced in Winnipeg, Man., in coopera-

Radio is an important aspect of evangelism. . . .

tion with Mennonite Brethren Communications, reach all corners of the Soviet Union from nine stations around the world.

These days you will find a number of other terms used to identify mission workers besides the traditional "missionary." That term now refers to a long-term worker appointed and fully supported by BOMAS at the invitation of a national church primarily for church and teaching ministries. A Christian Service worker is assigned to two years of work in Christian education, church ministries and community service. BOMAS provides transportation, medical, housing and food costs, as well as a small monthly allowance. These persons work primarily in evangelism and church planting abroad, with a view to possible long-term missionary service.

MAP (Missionary Assistance Program) is primarily a summer program, sometimes extending to longer periods. Workers pay their own transportation (often subsidized by churches and colleges) while BOMAS provides room and board and a monthly allowance. LIFE (Language Institute for Evangelism) is a MAP program in Japan, established to teach English to the Japanese through the Japanese Mennonite Brethren churches.

In 1984 BOMAS celebrated the centennial of the beginning of the mission effort of Mennonite Brethren, grateful to God for grace which has allowed this program to expand year by year with dedicated support of the constituency through both difficult and easy periods. The goal for the next hundred years continues to be expansion and strengthening of the church of Jesus Christ in all parts of the world, using not only workers from the traditional sending churches, but also workers from overseas congregations in their own home and even in a foreign mission program. The ultimate goal is a wholeness of ministry — to coordinate a ministry to physical needs through education, medicine, material and aid with evangelism.

A domestic Christian Service program in the United States provides anyone over the age of eighteen, including the retired, with a strong commitment to the lordship of Jesus Christ and a desire to share their faith an opportunity to join other such volunteers as members of church-planting teams, support personnel for young and emerging churches, Christian schools, rest homes, child care facilities, camps, and in physical work such as custodial work for church institutions. The opportunities are almost limitless.

While the greatest growth has been overseas, Mennonite Brethren have also enjoyed growth in America with extension northward in Manitoba, Alberta and British Columbia and eastward in Quebec in Canada. Urban centers such as Wichita, Denver, Fresno, San Jose, Vancouver, Saskatoon, Winnipeg, St. Catharines and Calgary have all experienced recent strong surges of growth. Anytime you are in one of these centers, take time to worship with a local Mennonite Brethren congregation.

FOR ADDITIONAL READING:

The Church in Mission edited by A.J. Klassen. Twenty-one essays focusing on the biblical foundations and historical recovery of the Christian mission. Published by the Board of Christian Literature, Fresno, Calif. (1967).

Mission Principles and Policies. A booklet outlining the theology and strategies of Mennonite Brethren Missions/Services.

Missions in the 80s. A working document which defines the directions which the Board of Missions/Services has set for this decade.

The Mustard Tree by Phyllis Martens. A good history of Mennonite Brethren missions until 1971. Published by the Board of Christian Literature, Fresno, Calif. (1971).

13
Growth through education and publishing

"Education is too important to be left solely to the educators," someone has said. Mennonite Brethren would agree. The education of young people, to not only make a living, but also to form a life, especially one that contributes to Christ's kingdom, has dominated the thinking of church leaders, parents and educators ever since the origin of the church. The spiritual revival in 1860 in southern Russia, which prompted the new Mennonite Brethren movement, began with the study of Scriptures, as did the spiritual movement during the Reformation from which the anabaptists emerged. Solid biblical teaching in the home, church and school has always been important to Mennonite Brethren.

Family nights, Sunday school, midweek programs, vacation Bible school, camping programs, youth retreats, church-sponsored high schools, Bible schools, Bible conferences, ministers' seminars, study conferences, colleges and a seminary are only part of the growing network of educational activities that have played a large role in Mennonite Brethren life and

86

thought in the last 130 years as the church has tried to fulfill its commission to "make disciples of all nations."

This emphasis on Christian education began informally in Russia with the appointment of itinerant ministers (sort of like American circuit riders), who went from place to place, stopping long enough to instruct, encourage and evangelize individuals or groups. They didn't marry, baptize or bury, however. Local ministers were expected to do those tasks. The itinerant minister's responsibility was spiritual care of the believers and evangelism of the unconverted. Names of these traveling preachers who continued the tradition in America often crop up in conversation today, for they provided some of the glue which held the entire body together as they moved from community to community, encouraging, admonishing, proclaiming and conveying information about new growth in one area to others and eliciting prayer support for needs. These itinerant ministers were held in common trust by everyone.

Bible study and fellowship meetings provided another setting for informal instruction in the Word. Men and women sat around the table with open Bibles before them to discuss a passage's interpretation and application to daily life. This basic understanding that Bible study must always be an activity of the entire body was applied to the corporate setting by arranging for Bible conferences, at which selected passages or a book of the Bible was studied, and where everyone was invited to participate freely.

In the early years of the church, children attended a type of Sunday school, which was more evangelical and devotional than instructional. The elders' main concern was to bring the children into the fold and to advise them how to live a holy life. Only later, in America, did the nature of Sunday school change, emphasizing biblical instruction for all — both young and old. All congregations have Sunday school classes today for all age groups.

Some scholars see the Bible school movement as one of the unique strengths of the Mennonite Brethren. Until the late sixties, about seventeen Bible schools of varying sizes flourished, some briefly, some for many years, in various parts of Canada and the United States. They drew young people into Bible study, especially for the winter months when farm work

Today the nature of Sunday school emphasizes biblical instruction for all. . . .

demanded less of their time. During wartime they also attracted young people wanting to sort out their beliefs on peace and nonresistance.

The Bible school movement began in 1878, only eighteen years after the founding of the Mennonite Brethren, to train Christian workers. The one distinctively Mennonite Brethren institution in South Russia was the Tschongraw Bible school in the Crimea, founded in 1918 and closed six years later in 1924 by government decree. The first Mennonite Brethren school in America was begun by educator J.F. Harms in the little community of Canada, Kan., in 1886, with classes in German, English and Bible. It survived for about four years. These early institutions and others like them either closed down, merged with another school, or evolved into another kind of institution.

But minor setbacks such as temporary closings or lack of funds didn't halt the early founders' determination to build institutions to train workers for Christ's service at home and in missions abroad. According to John B. Toews, the older generation recognized their task was to equip the younger generation to stand "against the dangers of our age," to preserve a Christian world view and to prepare them to serve the church. Teaching the young to recognize and be able to defend themselves against "worldliness" was extremely important.

In the middle 1980s three Bible institutes are still functioning. Each has a long, solid academic record and hundreds of graduates working in the home congregations, in overseas missions or in a lay witness through their professions. They are Bethany Bible Institute, Hepburn, Sask. (1927-); Winkler Bible Institute, Winkler, Man. (1925-) and Columbia Bible Institute, Clearbrook, B.C. (1945-), the latter sponsored jointly by Mennonite Brethren and General Conference Mennonites.

In addition, several academies, or high schools, continue to grow, providing youth with an education integrating faith and learning: Corn Bible Academy, Corn, Okla.(1902-); Immanuel High School, Reedley, Calif. (1912-); Mennonite Educational Institute, Clearbrook, B.C. (1944-); Mennonite Brethren Collegiate Institute, Winnipeg, Man., (1945-); Eden Christian College, Niagara-on-the-Lake, Ont. (1945-).

The move to offer young people a liberal arts education in a Christian setting began in 1904. By 1908 Tabor College and Academy in Hillsboro, Kan., opened its doors to students. Although Mennonite Brethren had begun and designed the institution, it was in fact owned, controlled and operated by a corporation until after the difficult years of the early 1930s when the General Conference took over its control. In 1944

Mennonite Brethren operate three Bible institutes and three four-year colleges in the U.S. and Canada. . . .

another school at Fresno was added, originally known as Pacific Bible Institute (now Fresno Pacific College), first operating as a Bible school, then as a two-year college, and later as a four-year liberal arts college. In 1979 ownership of both colleges was transferred to the district conferences.

In the mid-1940s the Canadian Mennonite Brethren, in response to a need for biblical studies at a post-high school level, started the Mennonite Brethren Bible College in Winnipeg. Then in 1955 the graduate department of theology at Tabor was transferred to Fresno, thus making possible the founding of the Mennonite Brethren Biblical Seminary. Twenty years later, the U.S. and Canadian churches agreed to sponsor it jointly.

The seminary has been thriving ever since as an accredited institution of theological education to prepare men and women for the Christian ministry. The purpose statement says in part: "The Seminary is committed to a biblio-centric curriculum. From the beginning of the Mennonite Brethren movement, the Scriptures have been accepted as the inspired Word of God, thus the sole authority in matters of faith and life. The Seminary is committed to the Scriptures as God's inspired and infallible Word. The school emphasizes biblical theology and challenges all students to build their life and philosophy upon a vital faith in Jesus Christ as Savior and Lord as interpreted by the Scriptures."

To preserve historical materials for research and writing, each of the three institutions of higher learning (Winnipeg, Fresno and Hillsboro) sponsors a Center for Mennonite Brethren Studies with a growing historical library and archives for persons interested in researching the roots of their denomination or individuals who were members of it.

This brief review of Mennonite Brethren educational efforts reveals that Mennonite Brethren are responsible for four post-high school institutions, as well as other institutions. A lot of schools and other kinds of institutions for a small conference of congregations to support? Well, yes, but Mennonite Brethren are like that. They like big challenges to serve the varied needs of all members of God's family. And if that isn't enough to work at, consider also the camping program, the active youth ministry (MBY), vacation Bible school, midweek programs, as well as home Bible studies.

Publishing also enjoys high priority among Mennonite Brethren. We like to publish. Mennonite Brethren were instrumental in the production of a Mennonite German-language newspaper, the *Mennonitische Rundschau*, which first appeared in 1880 and continues publication today under the auspices of the Canadian Conference. In 1885 the first Mennonite Brethren periodical was distributed, *Zionsbote* (Zion's Messenger), to be followed in 1937 by the English *Christian Leader*, edited at first for the youth of the conference and then later as the denominational organ. Next to join these on the production line were Sunday school materials for adults, and in Canada, a church organ for its members, now known as the *Mennonite Brethren Herald*. One of the main resource materials of adult Bible classes is the Mennonite Brethren *Adult Quarterly* (also available in German). We participate as a cooperative user in the inter-Mennonite Foundation Series Sunday school curriculum and the family worship manual, *REJOICE!*

Like most Mennonites, Mennonite Brethren like to sing. . . .

At present, a Board of Christian Literature for the General Conference and separate publications boards for the the Canadian and United States conferences oversees the tasks of producing needed church literature, coordinating publishing efforts of the two national conferences and encouraging writers. All publications are now offered to the public under the Kindred Press name. The various publications boards have produced books in many areas — history, theology, biography, fiction, hymnbooks, Sunday school materials, and missions. Some denominations considerably larger produce much less than the Mennonite Brethren. Clearly, we believe in publishing.

But here's another strength. Like most Mennonites, Mennonite Brethren love to sing a joyful song to the Lord. They can make the rafters in nearly any building loosen a little. Few congregations are without choirs and other kinds of singing groups, for good choral music is appreciated. Music is therefore an important part of the curriculum at our colleges, Bible schools and high schools. While you're waiting for the service to start some Sunday morning, browse through the Mennonite Brethren *Worship Hymnal* before you, which was first published in 1953. A supplement to it is in the planning stages.

For more information about any of these institutions or activities, write or phone them.

FOR ADDITIONAL READING:

Ewert, David. *Called to Teach*. Fresno, Calif.: Center of Mennonite Brethren Studies, 1980.

Klassen, A.J. *The Seminary Story*. Fresno, Calif.: Mennonite Brethren Biblical Seminary, 1975.

Prieb, Wesley J. and Don Ratzlaff. *To a Higher Plane of Vision: Tabor College — The First 75 Years*. Hillsboro, Kan.: Tabor College, 1983.

14
The inter-Mennonite connections

Sooner or later you will bump into other Mennonites, and there are thousands of them scattered all over Canada, the United States and many countries of the world. Mennonites are loosely joined in what is known as the Mennonite World Conference, which meets every six years in a different country. When it met in Wichita, Kan., in 1978, MWC president Million Belete, an Ethiopian who makes his home in Nairobi, Kenya, as regional secretary for the United Bible Societies of Africa, said, "Our gathering is a living example of part of the kingdom Christ established. We have come from different places. We speak different languages. We look different. Some of us are black, some white, some yellow. Some of us have curly hair, some straight. . . . We are members of the kingdom not because we are Puerto Ricans, Germans, Zairians, Indians or any other nationality. Neither can we even say we are his children because we are born of Christian parents, because God does not have any grandchildren. We must all be born again by regeneration."

The Wichita gathering registered 9,500 delegates from forty-four nations to celebrate the peoplehood of believers who

call themselves Mennonites. One observer called the conference a "populist affirmation of Mennonite unity, a celebration
not by theologians and bureaucrats but by the myriad and
diverse laypeople who compose the worldwide Mennonite mo-
saic." The order of the day at such a conference is not business
sessions, but worship and discussion of global issues facing the
Mennonite church in a changing and broken world. One world
conference speaker stressed that a Mennonite is not a believer
who sits tight on his or her heritage, clinging to safe structures, forms and phraseology, thereby remaining unproductive; but one who finds identity in the reality of the Cross and
becomes relevant to the present culture.

Is MWC the only formal connection Mennonite Brethren
have with other Mennonites? Not at all. Another important
one is Mennonite Central Committee (MCC), the over-arching
relief and development agency which draws support and personnel from most Mennonite bodies. MCC began in 1920 in
America as an effort to help fellow Mennonites in Russia suffering the effects of revolution, famine, disease and dislocation
following the Bolshevik revolution. P.C. Hiebert, Mennonite
Brethren educator and leader, played a key role in the founding and expansion of this relief and service agency, serving as
its chairman for thirty-three years.

MCC takes its mandate from Luke 4:18 in which Christ
defines his task as "to preach good news to the poor . . . to
proclaim release to the captives and recovery of sight to the
blind, to set at liberty those who are oppressed." Sixteenth-cen-
tury Mennonite leader Menno Simons explained his faith in
this way: "True evangelical faith cannot lie dormant; it clothes
the naked; it feeds the hungry; it comforts the sorrowful; it
shelters the destitute; it serves those that harm it; it binds up
that which is wounded. It has become all things to all men."
Through Mennonite Central Committee (MCC) the Mennonite
faith community seeks to become all things to people of all
races, nationalities and social groups.

Freeing people "in the name of Christ," the motto of MCC,
takes many forms from "liberation from poverty, disease, illiteracy and malnutrition to liberty from unproductive penal systems, social injustice, hatred and war or from the get-ahead
North American rat race to a simpler life-style." Perhaps cen-

turies of persecution in Europe and feelings of inferiority there
and in other countries have caused Mennonites to identify with
oppressed people. The concern is obviously there and their con-
tribution recognized widely.

MCC invites committed Christians, young and old, to join
in the battle against poverty, disease, illiteracy, malnutrition
and injustice in the name of Christ through two or three-year
assignments in close to fifty countries around the world with
a total budget reaching nearly $25 million dollars. It functions
as a kind of clearing house for such concerns, drawing financial
and moral support from all who wish to participate in its programs. Of MCC's 950 workers, about 100 are Mennonite Breth-

*MCC invites committed Christians, young and old, to join in the battle
against poverty, disease, illiteracy, malnutrition and injustice in the
name of Christ. . . .*

ren volunteers serving as agriculturalists, engineers, teachers, nurses and community workers, all answering Christ's call to love God and all people and promote a better life from local churches to foreign countries.

A subsidiary agency of MCC is Mennonite Disaster Service, an international organization which stands ready to help anyone struck by disaster of any kind, natural or provoked by human failure. Name the disaster, big or small, and MDS volunteers soon arrive on the scene to sort through and clear away debris, mud out and scrub down homes, rebuild and repair, and get the victims back on their feet as soon as possible.

Attempts have been made to explain the mystique of this volunteer movement, which shows no signs of diminishing and whose presence in the midst of disaster continues to cause victims to feel a strange, bewildered, but grateful thanks for the

Name the disaster, big or small, and MDS volunteers soon arrive on the scene to get the victims back on their feet as soon as possible. . . .

assistance. To donate free time and labor with no demand for financial reward makes no sense in a world controlled by money. MDSers give time — from one day to several months; they give energy — sometimes long, back-breaking hours; they give a listening ear; and they give love.

While MDS began about thirty years ago primarily as a men's organization, today young people, women and retired persons are all invited to make MDS their vehicle for expressing their loving concern for others because of their faith in Christ. How many different kinds of Mennonites are involved? I don't know. MDSers don't discuss denominational fences. MDS has been described by some as the Third Movement in the church, bridging the gap between the scholar in the ivory tower and the complacent church member. It has been referred to as Mennonites Doing Something, Modern Day Samaritans and even the Mennonite Diaconate Service. There's a spot in it for you any time.

But even that isn't the only connection with other Mennonites. The Mennonite family in many localities joins to sponsor enormous, colorful and exhilarating MCC relief sales. People bring together food, quilts and handcrafted articles of all kinds, and then invite friends and neighbors to join them in eating, visiting and celebrating the goodness of God but also to share of their plenty to make life easier for the poor and needy. A sizable portion of MCC funds is raised in this way, and the movement is growing, for it's a unique opportunity for like-minded people to cooperate in a venture which seems to have no limits to its potential.

Another booming enterprise in which Mennonite Brethren cooperate with other Mennonites is the network of Selp-Help and Thrift Shops operated in communities with a large enough concentration of Mennonites to provide necessary staffing. Beautiful and carefully made handicrafts from overseas countries are sold to provide increased income for nationals in these countries, many of which have weak economies.

Another important role other Mennonites play in the life and work of Mennonite Brethren is through the Peace Section, a body which monitors political legislation as it relates to Mennonite concerns of peace and nonresistance. During critical international crises, Mennonites have joined through Peace Section to negotiate with governments to provide alternative service to the military for their young men and provide counseling regarding registration and conscription.

Mennonites, including Mennonite Brethren, have also cooperated in such efforts as a mutual aid society, mental health agencies, homes for the elderly, and some publishing.

But where Mennonites have never quite been able to join together has been in educational and publishing efforts. Each member of the Mennonite family has its own colleges, headquarters, periodicals and missions organization, though this doesn't mean they don't consult with each other. The Council of Mission Board Secretaries (COMBS) meets regularly for consultation, as do the editors of church periodicals and other church leaders.

You may sense that Mennonite Brethren unity with other Mennonites is not strongly apparent at the congregational level with regard to peace and nonresistance issues, social ethics and relationship to the state. MBs, born in the cradle of the pietistic movement in southern Russia partly as a reaction to lax spiritual life and authoritarian leadership, are oriented to their past history in their concern for biblical truth (What does the Word say?) and in their stance of separatism from other Mennonites. Having broken away from a group once, they still carry a fear — sometimes unspoken, sometimes voiced — of losing doctrinal purity if they don't remain aloof from those they once left.

As I checked the literature on the subject, I found repeated mention of this hesitancy, much of it for wrong reasons. The late J.A. Toews, historian and theologian, wrote we forget too readily that the renewal movement which began in the Mennonite church and led to the secession of a minority group continued to influence and change the larger body from which Mennonite Brethren seceded. Moreover, the General Conference of Mennonites in America, which has sometimes felt the greatest ostracism, does not have its historical roots in Russian Mennonitism of the 19th century, but is the result of a church movement in this continent, and many of their congregations are closer in spirit and practice to the Mennonite Brethren of 1860 than to the Mennonite church in Russia of 1860. He called for a basic reorientation toward other Mennonites, for at times the emphasis on "separation" from the world has deteriorated into an isolation from other Christians, especially Mennonite Christians. He saw closer inter-Mennonite working relationships resulting in our rediscovering and strengthening many aspects of our spiritual heritage.

This attitude is breaking down at many levels, however, and showing itself in an increasing readiness to join in more inter-Mennonite activities as listed above. Those Mennonite Brethren, especially church leaders — but also laypersons — who have much opportunity to fellowship with other Mennonites, can't understand some of the hesitancy to reach across in full fellowship. Because the Kauffman-Harder study of the belief and doctrine of Mennonite and Brethren in Christ churches reveals that the members of the five groups are more alike in orthodoxy than they are different (the main denominator in our common faith is the confession of Christ's lordship), Mennonite Brethren would benefit spiritually if they recognized the genuine Christianity found in many other denominations, including Mennonites, and that we, too, suffer from imperfections. Prejudgment, unconscious though it may be, is always the beginning of more serious prejudice.

MB, GC, EMB, EMC, EMMC, OM — put them all together, they certainly don't spell "Mother" or even "Mennonite," or One Family. This section of this chapter has been difficult to write, for we cannot disregard the existence of thousands of other Mennonites with great spiritual vitality and outreach without hurting ourselves. But on the other hand, it is also important not to disregard the concern of Mennonite Brethren who don't want to be dumped into a common denominator. Our need, or perhaps better said, our yearning for a strong separate spiritual identity, an attitude which has been with us from the time of our origin, has sometimes been to our advantage and sometimes a hindrance. But the lesson we are learning slowly but surely is that God's Word does not permit this generation to allow Grandpa's and Great-grandma's attitudes to determine present thinking and action. Mennonite Brethren have much to offer others. Other Mennonites have much to offer us.

The following is not a game of anagrams, but a little help

for newcomers who get caught in Mennonite institutional mazes and can't find their way out.

MCC — Mennonite Central Committee

MDS — Mennonite Disaster Service

MWC — Mennonite World Conference

VS — Voluntary service

CO — A conscientious objector to war

CPS — Civilian Public Service

COMBS — Council of Mission Board Secretaries

MEDA — Mennonite Economic Development Associates

MMAA — Mennonite Mutual Aid Association

Meetinghouse — Cooperating group of Mennonite and Brethren in Christ editors

CIM — Council of International Ministries

MMHS — Mennonite Mental Health Services

MNA — Mennonite Nurses Association

IPF — Inter-Collegiate Peace Fellowship

And dozens of others!

FOR ADDITIONAL READING:

Dyck, Cornelius J., Ed. "The Mennonite Central Committee Story Series": *From the Files of MCC* (1980); *Responding to Worldwide Needs* (1980); *Witness and Service in North America* (1980); *Something Meaningful for God: The Stories of Some Who Served with MCC* . . . (1981); *MCC Experiences: Issues and Choices* (1982). All published by Herald Press, Scottdale, Pa.

Wiebe, Katie Funk, *Day of Disaster*. Scottdale, Pa.: Herald Press, 1976.

15
Growing a vision

It's time to end our conversation about the Mennonite Brethren. I could have said much more, but that would have required a much longer writing. I hope you'll take time to look into some of the books listed at the end of most chapters. So far I've been describing the church of the past and the present. What lies ahead for the Mennonite Brethren? To write about the future always means checking with the past, for the future always grows out of what has happened.

In 1960 Mennonite Brethren celebrated the centennial of the founding of the Mennonite Brethren Church. Hundreds of words were written at the time about "Our Christian Heritage," "Statement of Mennonite Brethren Position," "Call to Thanksgiving, Prayer and Repentance," "Centennial Conferences Express Repentance for Unbrotherly Feelings, Words, Deeds," and so forth. In 1974 Mennonites celebrated another centennial — their coming to the Great Plains area of the United States in the 1870s. Once again we asked: "What have we gained during our years in America? What are the shaping influences of the past which have contributed to our present condition? What accounts for our attitudes toward God, the Bible, church life, missions, work, leisure, ideas of success and

101

satisfaction? What has been our heritage? What is our specific task for the future? What does God expect of us?"

The answer to the first group of questions comes as we look at ourselves, our church, our conference, personal friends and friends of the church. We have officially retained the name "Mennonite Brethren" although some congregations have set it aside. We have many beautiful, sometimes ornate and elaborate church sanctuaries, and substantial budgets for faithwork at home and abroad. We have new hymnbooks, new constitutions, a fairly recently revised statement of faith, new choir robes, fresh flowers before the pulpit each Sunday, regular bulletins and church newsletters, expanding Christian education departments and youth ministries, church offices, public address systems, paved parking lots, air conditioning, pipe organs, cushioned pews. . . .

These are a few of the outward symbols of our present condition, these and the things out of sight in archives, attics, cupboards and memories: King James Bibles, common cups, Christian Endeavor, revival meetings, Golden Texts, attendance banners, green divider curtains strung on wires, and prayer meetings at which most present prayed audibly. Let's not forget *Faspa* (the traditional German light lunch), and riverside baptisms, horse-drawn buggies and kneeling for prayer. They were also part of our condition at one time and slipped away gradually with popularized theological terms like "Let go and let God," and "He saves, he keeps, he satisfies," and all-day missions festivals, "correspondences" in church journals from missionaries abroad, informal family weddings, and head coverings for women. All of these were important at one time.

Our church history books tell us that while all these details, large and small, important and unimportant, were weaving in and out of our daily personal and corporate experience, we felt fairly confident our doctrine was Bible-centered, with a strong emphasis on personal regeneration, discipleship and missions, and that we tolerated freedom of spiritual expression.

Some of the young among us and those who join our congregations from other ethnic, religious or social backgrounds sometimes accept the name Mennonite Brethren as merely on par with any other mainstream denominational tag. They have a hard time understanding the intense emotion sometimes still aroused when questions of ethnic background are brought up, such as "Does a strong emotional attachment with an ethnic identity hamper either personal or corporate spiritual growth?" These questioners probably do not realize that when the Mennonites came to America, they were non-English speaking settlers who faced many new customs and were naturally fearful of strangers. Particularly, they feared being swallowed by this strange new culture and losing the identity they had forged at great price in other lands. It might have helped our forebears to know that the people among whom they were settling were also afraid of being swallowed by the Mennonites. This large close-knit group of spiritually zealous, hard-working, thrifty God-loving settlers also intimidated their neighbors. The neighbors feared their land might be over-taken by these newcomers who didn't seem to know when the sun had gone down and it was time to rest.

The effect, however, of this early discomfort has been that some Mennonites now want to shed the historical past at a time when other evangelical traditions are seriously refocus-ing on theirs more surely to give them clearer direction for the rough road through the eighties. Theologian J.B. Toews writes that "a people who neglect to recognize God's hand in their history lose consciousness of their calling. They fail to praise God for the love, mercy and kindness extended to their forebears and to the present generation of God's people." Not always have we recognized soon enough that ethnic conscious-ness will not halt church growth if a group sees itself as part of the larger body of Christians, rather than as the whole. The past, all of it, is always our own past. We can allow it to ballast our progress, it is true, but it can also serve as a springboard into a brighter future.

Early Mennonite Brethren struggled with another fear — a tension they brought with them from Russia not washed away by the waters of the Atlantic — the tension with the Mennonite church (*Kirchliche* or churchly group) out of whose midst they broke away in Russia. This fear of inter-Mennonite fellowship, which the 1960 Centennial began to speak to, still lurks in the shadows of church life occasionally. At various times this fear has hindered home mission work and fellowship with other Mennonite groups, but hasn't been strong enough to allow us to shed our Mennonite identity and move over fully into the mainstream of evangelicalism. Along with other churches in America, Mennonite Brethren suffered a loss of spiritual vitality in the seventies through the gradually increasing institutionalization of the church, a trend not recognized immediately for its leeching power. The development of budgets, programs, buildings and executive secretaries seemed to bring denominational success even if it encouraged us to relax our pilgrim status in society. Urbanization, with its erosion of traditional values and culture, revealed our theological convictions to ourselves (which was a strengthening factor), but also exposed our prejudices (which should bring us to our knees, but hasn't entirely).

The study done by Howard Kauffman and Leland Harder, published in *Anabaptists Four Centuries Later*, showed that in comparison with five other Mennonite bodies the Mennonite Brethren placed first in Bible knowledge but last in ethical-social concern. Why? Thrifty, hard-working, educationally minded Mennonite Brethren are most likely to belong to middle to upper middle-class income groups with a large percentage of professionals and businesspersons. That, and the current push into a strong individualism (despite our simple immigrant origins in this land) has made identification with the poor and oppressed, particularly of this country, sometimes difficult. It doesn't come naturally. The Spirit of Christ needs to teach us. We want to be open.

Mennonite Brethren, who came to North America knowing it was a Protestant land, now must face the fact that they are part of a pluralistic society in which Protestantism is only one of many belief systems. We are being forced to decide how to relate to the great North American evangelical movement, with its emphasis on religious television programming, large-scale churches and sometimes strong strains of nationalism. But the urgency of the nuclear arms race also demands we clear the way to finding better ways to express our faith in acts of peace and reconciliation. The present situation demands a clear response from everyone, even those for whom the peace witness is new.

Along with North American society as a whole, Mennonite Brethren have also experienced the pressures of the human rights movement of the seventies. We, too, have felt the push of the young for more relevance in church, the demands of minorities and women for equal recognition of their gifts, and the pressure to become more involved in programs which bring social action and evangelism into one package. To find answers to these questions has had its rugged moments.

Yet to look pessimistically at the present condition of the Mennonite Brethren would do us all an injustice. All kinds of vitalities can be found within our congregations for which we can be grateful. Church attendance and membership remains stable or is growing slightly. Young people remain vitally interested in conference youth activities and voluntary service. Local congregations are moving toward inter-Mennonite cooperation in a number of projects. Interest in missions remains high. Church planting in metropolitan areas, particularly among ethnic groups is gaining new impetus from many areas. Publishing ventures and higher education retain strong support from the constituency. Stewardship remains at consistently high levels.

Theologian Waldo Hiebert writes, "While we cannot see a deep and general renewal across the brotherhood, there are 'pockets' of renewal: churches that are reaching out to neighbors, spontaneous Bible study and prayer groups, mutual caring and sharing, new forms of worship, more joy and praise in the services and daily life, community concern, new awareness for the need of personal meditation and communion with God, and lay witness. These are signs that the Spirit is seeking to lead us to new life, new forms, new ministries in the world." For these signs we are grateful to God.

Theologian Howard Loewen writes that the challenge before the Mennonite Brethren community is to "grow a vision" for our future life together. We must "possess the maturity to grow beyond our present stature and thinking." According to Loewen, this will include:

(a) A growing awareness of our historical and spiritual roots in the broader Christian tradition.

(b) A movement toward a more wholistic view of the gospel, not preoccupation with only a few favorite doctrines like conversion, virgin birth and inerrancy.

(c) A greater acknowledgment of the social dimension of Jesus's gospel, including warfare, racism, poverty and other issues as well as a more mature understanding of the church's relation to the political arena and greater ethical understanding of our faith.

(d) A greater understanding that while spiritual rebirth is basic to the gospel, it must also be accompanied by an equal emphasis on spiritual discipline of the inner life, the life in the Spirit.

(e) A continual emphasis on the importance of Scripture, yet an emphasis which sees the practical and experiential nature of its message rather than viewing it primarily as a source book of doctrine.

(f) More openness to other Christian traditions rather than building walls around our own.

Other church leaders add that the new vision will include the greater emergence of the laity in the life and ministry of the church (no person will be unemployed in God's kingdom), closer relationships within the church community, the return of biblical preaching, an emphasis on spiritual gifts and their ministries, and the desire for a simpler, less luxurious lifestyle as the result of having worked through the theology of affluence to reflect obedience to Christ. The church will see its responsibility to share more deeply in human suffering and need and prophetically call attention to human needs while fulfilling the mandate to spread the gospel. Part of this response will include mobilizing to meet the needs of families in crisis. If Mennonite Brethren accept this challenge, they have great things to look forward to as they continue the work of Christ.

Certainly the future of the Mennonite Brethren looks bright if the faith-life becomes an invigorating way of life instead of a habit; if we allow the Bible to speak to all aspects of our condition today — divorce and abortion, drug addiction, arguments between neighbors, suffering and death, energy crises, inflation and nuclear threats; and if, in Loewen's words, we can accept ourselves "as a particular, authentic representation of God's people" that is part of the larger evangelical spirit (but only a part) and also a part of another church tradition with roots in the anabaptist-Mennonite movement of the 16th century.

Changes in church structures for the eighties are certain, writes seminary president Elmer Martens, some because society is changing, others because a renewed church will reorganize to accommodate new priorities of life and witness.

By the ever-present mercy of God through Jesus Christ, in the years ahead Mennonite Brethren will develop new forms for a different age. Experimentation may be necessary for a while, but a deeper recognition will emerge that forms of worship, methods of evangelism and missions and stewardship are expressions of relationships with God and other persons, and that these must change as times change. And then God will be glorified as the power of the Holy Spirit is reflected in our lives. We invite you to grow the vision with us, for "where there is no vision, the people perish" (Prov. 29:18).